ANXIETY
and the Gift of Imagination

ANXIETY
and the Gift of Imagination

Robin Alter, PhD

A new model for helping parents and children manage anxiety

Published by Alter Psychology Professional Corporation
The Promenade, Suite 301A
1 Promenade Circle
Thornhill, Ontario L4J 4P8

Cover illustration by Paul Madonna

ISBN-13: 978-1466432062
ISBN-10: 1466432063

Contents

Acknowledgements

My first thanks must go to my clients, the children and parents who inspired me with their unique approach to life and its inherent problems. You are the reason I decided to write this book. By allowing me to help you, you have helped me more than you realize. I particularly want to express my appreciation to those parents who returned to my office especially to thank me for finding a way to relieve their child's anxiety.

For their many insightful suggestions, I am indebted to my intelligent and generous friends and family: Lonnie Barbach, Marcia Meyers, Nancy Packard, Sharon Gordetsky, Rhoda Payne, Zailig Pollock, Chris Littlefield, Charlotte Danard, Gabe Pollock, Ronnie and Diane Alter, and others.

My gratitude runs deep for everyone at Hincks-Dellcrest Children's Centre in Toronto and Blue Hills Child and Family Centre in Aurora, Ontario, with whom I have been working for over thirty years. Thank you for creating a climate of trust and mutual support, which permitted the ideas of this book to germinate. Hincks-Dellcrest also assisted me in my research on anxiety and imagination in children, as did Irene Bevc, Lisa Dang, Dr. Debby Zweig, and staff members at York Central Hospital Anxiety Disorders Clinic.

I am indebted to Dr. Paul Harris of Harvard University for taking the time to discuss with me the plausibility of my ideas and for encouraging me to pursue them. Dr. Harris's rigorous work on the imagination has given us a much greater understanding of this critical aspect of the human experience.

I am especially grateful to my illustrator, John Strachan, who sadly is no longer with us. You will find a tribute to John at the end of this book. And, for stepping in at the eleventh hour to create the masterful illustration for the cover, I thank Paul Madonna, an artist from San Francisco. This book would have been difficult to complete without Didi Pollock, whose capable hands guided the project to a final result of which I am very proud.

I also owe a debt of gratitude to my late parents, my dad, Murray Alter, who always said I should believe in myself, and my mom, Lee Alter, who was my role model for courage. And finally, I could never have written this book without Martin Yaffe, my husband, partner and best friend, whose love is always backed up by action and who makes every day worthwhile.

Robin Alter

What this book is about

CHILDREN WHO SUFFER FROM ANXIETY are typically regarded by others as scaredy-cats – inadequate, deficient in courage, and unable to look life squarely in the eye. Certainly this is how they see themselves. But despite the unhappiness experienced by anxious children, usually it is their parents who seek help, often having to coerce the child to come and see a professional like me. The child can't see the point in talking to anyone about the problem because he is firmly convinced that no one will be able to help him face life's challenges and simply feel normal. In fact, children in this situation commonly deny that there is a problem. The child's solution is simple – avoid whatever is causing the anxiety and that dreaded feeling disappears, at least for the moment. Since most children don't think beyond the present moment, that's good enough for them.

However, when the child is brought into my office, she is forced to confront the issue and often appears to be filled with shame, which is sometimes revealed more through body language than in words. Our eyes rarely meet. The child may try to hide by retreating inside her hat or slumping down into her shirt, or by facing the wall and away from me as I try to make contact.

Yet, in my clinical practice and research I have discovered something rather remarkable – that anxiety is nothing to be ashamed of. In fact, anxiety is more often than not the spin-off of a vivid imagination, the source of our creative impulses. For some children, the vividness of the images they conjure up makes it hard for them to distinguish imagination from reality. Other children may be aware that what they imagine is not real, and yet they still feel great anxiety. But in my experience, whether or not children can distinguish the imaginary from the real, the way to relieve their anxiety is to teach them to control the imagination. It's really much like riding a bicycle: if you couldn't brake or steer effectively, you'd be in a lot of trouble. Once we show children that anxiety is often caused by an out-of-control imagination, then we can find a way to help them manage their fears and avoid being saddled with a negative label such as anxiety disorder!

In making the connection between anxiety and an overactive imagination, I certainly do not mean to minimize the seriousness of your child's anxiety. Trying to talk your child out of his or her experience by saying "Oh, you're just imagining that" will likely lead to one big power struggle. I hope that this book will help you and your child to understand the imagination, to respect its power, and finally to achieve a more peaceful alliance with it.

Everyone experiences anxieties, but in its more extreme forms, anxiety can dominate family life. Children with anxiety refuse to go on family outings, balk at entering a restaurant, miss school or cause a parent to miss work. They have tantrums and meltdowns, doing whatever they can to control the situation and keep anxiety at bay. In their attempts to find solutions, parents blame themselves or each other. Anxieties range from the common fears of darkness, dogs or other animals, being alone, burglars, insects, clowns, performance at school and elsewhere, to less commonly experienced phobias such as germs, bathrooms, dining out, elevators, thunderstorms, ghosts, and so on.

In Canada and the U.S., estimates of the number of children with problem anxiety range from about 6% to about 13% – that is, as many as one in eight children under the age of eighteen may suffer from this debilitating condition. At the children's mental health centre where I work and where, in the outpatient department alone, more than 500 children receive help each year, the incidence of anxiety-related problems in children has increased from 19% to 29% of our clients over the past ten years. This problem is extensive and growing, but that is only part of the story. In addition, there are untold numbers of children whose functioning is compromised by anxiety but who are not being seen by therapists, either because their parents are disinclined to seek help or because their suffering isn't deemed severe enough. There are many children who don't meet the criteria for anxiety disorder, but who are, nevertheless, suffering needlessly from excessive anxiety. These children are hanging on, moving from one fear to another, distracted and not reaching their potential.

For parents with children who suffer from anxiety, this is the book you've been waiting for. *Anxiety and the Gift of Imagination* sets the record straight on what anxiety is, how it can be triggered by an overactive imagination, and how it can take over a young person's life. Most importantly, the book provides parents with specific tools for helping their children master their thoughts and imaginations and keep their anxiety in check and so achieve more control over their lives.

This book is intended not only for families, but it also for therapists, offering them a unique and helpful way to think about anxiety. It will explain why many current standard therapies do not work as well for children as they do for adults.

Indeed, there is a gap in the resources available for helping people deal with anxiety which *Anxiety and the Gift of Imagination* aims to fill. Currently, there are many popular books for adults that teach that controlling one's mind is the key to being in control of one's life. Eckhart Tolle's *A New Earth: Awakening to Your Life's Purpose* is one example. A growing number of adults are learning this new skill, finding relief from stress, and achieving more contentment and even joyfulness in the process. Unfortunately, there is very little help of this kind for children. *Anxiety and the Gift of Imagination* explains how children's minds differ from adults' and presents, in a clear manner, ways to approach children, so they can learn the tools necessary for controlling their minds and imaginations, and thus avoid years of distress.

A cautionary note: while the approach detailed here has proved helpful for many children in my practice, it is not intended for every single child who is excessively anxious. Sometimes anxiety is a piece of a more pervasive problem, such as autism. Because children with autism often have poor imaginative capabilities, it is unlikely that they would respond favourably to this approach. However, when dealing with less imaginative children who are not on the autism spectrum, I have found ways to adapt the basic concepts to their needs as well.

I have been working as a psychologist for more than thirty years, treating children and adolescents with a broad range of psychological and behaviour problems, ranging from severe anxieties to conduct disorders, learning disabilities, problems with bullying, ADHD, etc. For twenty-nine years, I have been a consulting psychologist at a large children's mental health centre in Toronto, where I have met with more than 10,000 children and families, many of whom have suffered from anxiety. This has led me to develop the Imagination/Anxiety Model, which I have used successfully to resolve anxiety disorders for hundreds of my private practice clients. I know through experience how to communicate with children in a manner that is effective and engaging. The response to my approach has been overwhelmingly positive.

In addition to my clinical work, I have taught psychology at York University for over twenty years and am also a frequently requested public speaker in the community on topics such as anxiety, ADHD, bullying, psychological assessment, cognitive behaviour therapy with children, and how to communicate with children about their learning disabilities. I have made numerous television and radio appearances and have been published in newspapers and magazines. I have also given many workshops and presentations to mental health professionals and teachers, and at public and private schools in Canada and the U.S.

How I came to write this book

I BEGAN TO THINK ABOUT THE CONNECTION between imagination and anxiety many years ago, when Melanie, a delightful eleven-year-old girl, entered my office. (The names of all the clients mentioned in this book have been changed to protect their privacy.) For all the world, Melanie looked like a happy child, with big, curious hazel eyes, a toothy grin and a scattering of freckles. But Melanie was anything but carefree. She suffered from debilitating anxiety, which she experienced in the form of severe stomach aches. Her anxiety was so intense that it was excruciatingly painful for Melanie to get herself out the door every weekday for school. She also missed many social events, such as parties and sleepovers. Yet her grades were good, and she had positive friendships with other children. She was articulate, and most people would have considered her more mature than the average eleven-year-old.

I really enjoyed my discussions with Melanie. I asked her what else she liked to do, besides spending time with her friends and family. Her eyes sparkled as she told me about her art. She painted with watercolours and oils, and she described in great, enthusiastic detail the paintings she was so proud of. As I listened, I wondered out loud, "Do you think there's any connection between your incredible creativity and your anxiety?"

Melanie stopped, looked at me, perplexed but clearly interested. I continued, "Well, Melanie, it seems to me you don't just have a fear of something. When you imagine something, you imagine it in full colour, with loads of detail, and it becomes a very realistic and elaborate scene." She nodded eagerly. "Yes," she said. "That's how I see things. I can picture all the details so clearly. It's like I'm really there."

Sitting with Melanie all those years ago, I didn't know what to make of this epiphany – was this case common or unique? But I was intrigued, and so I continued to ask questions and to search for answers. On that day, my research began to follow a new path.

From then on, I incorporated new questions into my interviews with parents of children suffering from anxiety. The answer to the question: "Does your child have a highly developed imagination?" always came back a resounding, "Yes!" And often the kids would respond with, "And sometimes it gets me into big trouble. I imagine the most awful things!"

My young patients were eager to recount in vivid detail how they flexed their imaginations. Some kids have extremely imaginative play, making up wonderfully elaborate scenarios and acting them out with their dolls or action figures. Older kids write stories or plays, and some compose songs, often with intricate lyrics. Other kids express their imaginations through art, creating complex, detailed drawings and

paintings. Still others build elaborate structures with Lego, building blocks or clay. The realm of the imagination really is limitless and takes many different forms, but the children who came to see me for anxiety all typically shared one common characteristic: these were children gifted with highly active and developed imaginations. Furthermore, although they were no less mature than other children, these highly imaginative children often continued with imaginative play long after many children of their age had given it up.

After years of research and clinical observation in my office, I was able to confirm the validity of the theory that had dawned on me so long ago with Melanie, that anxiety in children often results from a vivid and overactive imagination. Although having a highly developed imagination is usually considered to be a natural talent and something to be enjoyed and celebrated, if the imagination is unchecked and allowed to go off in any direction it pleases, it can lead the person down a path toward anxiety and extreme distress. Since my experience with Melanie, I have dedicated myself to researching tools to help these children tame and control their imaginations, so that they can live happy, creative and less stressful lives.

Different tools work for different children. The anxious kids that I've helped in my practice are not only different from children who present with problems other than excessive anxiety, but, because of their creativity, they are also different from one another. Some of them already have a measure of control over their imagination; others have very little. Over the years, I have assembled a collection of tools and strategies, some that are recommended by professionals in the field and some that were created by the children themselves. Indeed, most of the children I have seen in my practice seem to prefer putting their own stamp on things, and generally each of my clients develops his or her one-of-a-kind tools for gaining better control of the imagination.

I hope that after reading this book, parents and kids will share their experiences on my website, www.docrobin.com. In sharing our experiences, we all learn. Certainly, this book was inspired by what I learned from all the wonderful children and families who sought my help over the years. Although I have worked in this field for a long time, I expect to continue learning from the comments of people who read this book and experiment with my approach. If we share our successes with one another, more and more children can grow up with a carefree enjoyment of their imagination.

How this book is organized

I FELT THE BEST PLACE TO START was by trying to sort out normal levels of anxiety from those that are truly debilitating. Living in an age of anxiety, we have all come to accept a certain level of stress as the price of being alive, and our kids are not exempt from this condition. In Chapter 1, I have tried to pin down when anxiety levels are simply too much for a child to bear on his own or her own and when to intercede. In Chapter 2, I discuss how the mind works and especially how children's minds differ from those of adults. In Chapter 3, I begin to explain how an over-active imagination often produces anxiety.

Chapter 4 deals with helping children to think constructively about the future. Being able to anticipate the future is certainly a useful cognitive tool, but many anxious children tend to think too much about the future. They are always imagining all the terrible things that might happen, and they have too little experience to properly evaluate what is likely to happen and what is unlikely or even impossible. We need to give our children tools for evaluating what is real or likely, unlikely or even impossible. We all take risks. We gather information from credible sources, we take precautions, and we venture forward. In this chapter, I discuss how to teach our kids this important life skill.

In Chapter 5, I tackle the issue of putting busy minds to rest at the end of the day and getting a good night's sleep. This can be a challenge for children with active imaginations, but it can be done.

In Chapter 6, I take all the lessons of the previous chapters and put them into the form of a step-by-step manual, so that you can apply what you have learned and talk with your child about fears and anxieties in a way that will be validating for them and truly helpful.

Chapter 7 is about the role of tools and strategies. I sincerely hope you resist the urge to skip right to this chapter. The tools and strategies might be helpful, but they will be more beneficial if they are put in the context of an overall understanding of the imagination/anxiety connection.

Chapters 8 and 9 are addressed directly to children. Some of the children I've seen in my practice – even children barely able to read a first grade primer – have tried to struggle through the articles I've written for professionals and for parent magazines. Many children find themselves looking for help on the internet and often find themselves on pharmaceutical sites. They come into my office asking for a certain medication to quell their anxious feelings. These chapters are for all the children who have been searching by themselves for different ways of dealing with their anxiety.

Chapter 10 tackles why my method works for many children, why it may not work for all, and what to do when it doesn't work.

Throughout the book, you will find many fine illustrations by the gifted John Strachan. John told me, after reading the book four times, that it had "become his bible." I hope many others find it even half as useful. Since I believe that children and even many adults who suffer from anxiety tend to be more imaginative than most people and possibly have a more developed visual sense, I felt it only fitting that this book have a strong visual component. I have been privileged to have John as my illustrator.

Chapter 1

When anxiety becomes a problem

MANY PARENTS BELIEVE that childhood is a carefree and innocent time, that since children are spared the responsibilities of adulthood, they have little to worry about. This couldn't be further from the truth. Many parents also believe that by being the best parent they can be, they can shelter their children from the frightening aspects of growing up, and, if they do their job properly, their children will spend their days playing joyfully.

This chapter explains what anxiety is and how to tell normal anxiety from problem anxiety. The emergence of anxiety and of the ability to overcome it are closely linked to the stages of a child's intellectual development. Many childhood anxieties are normal, and children typically outgrow them. However parents should be concerned if anxieties persist beyond the normal stage or if they interfere significantly with the child's daily life.

Why then do so many children worry about every little thing? As we become adults, most of us naturally lose our fear of the things that frightened us as children. When we were kids, we may have been afraid of the dark, the basement or something under the bed, but most of us put these things behind us long before we leave childhood. Some children, however, no matter how often they are told not to worry, persist in this unhappy activity, which puts a damper on everything and robs them of much pleasure and fun.

How can you, as a parent, determine when normal childhood fears turn into a more serious problem? How can you best understand your

FEAR

child's fears? How can you avoid blaming yourself, when, in spite of your best efforts, those fears persist? How can you help your child be less burdened by worries? What exactly is anxiety and how can we best deal with it? To answer these questions, we must first understand the difference between plain old fear and anxiety. Let's get started.

Fear and anxiety: How are they different?

FEAR IS A NORMAL AND SENSIBLE RESPONSE to something or someone that could realistically cause harm. It's an unpleasant, agitated feeling accompanied by physical symptoms like a rapid heart rate, sweating and possibly a stomach ache and nausea. Disturbing though it may be, fear has an important and useful purpose. Can you even imagine not being afraid of someone who is pointing a gun in your direction? Of course not! And what else should you feel when riding in a car with a drunk or reckless driver? If we didn't experience fear, it would be almost impossible to avoid hazards and injury. Life would be one catastrophe after another!

The fear response is called anxiety when a person is having the same kinds of physical symptoms that people have when they are afraid, but the response is to events or things that are not dangerous or are much less harmful than the person imagines. A good example of this is claustrophobia, when someone is afraid of closed spaces and is

ANXIETY

unable to breathe or has the feeling of walls collapsing and crushing them. The person in distress will be able to tell you that she knows logically that she is not really in danger, but her body is reacting in the moment as if the walls really were about to close in and she actually was going to suffocate. It's not hard to find other examples of situations that may cause anxiety: speaking to an audience, driving on a busy highway or making a routine visit to the dentist. These may be unpleasant experiences, but, if considered logically, not nearly as bad as when they are amplified by the person suffering from anxiety.

How is it different for children?

DESPITE MANY PARENTS' SUNNY VIEW OF CHILDHOOD, the reality is that children tend to have many more fears and anxieties than adults. They share many of their parents' fears but also have many fears of their own. Your child has had less experience with the world than you and therefore has not had the same opportunities to discover what is truly harmful and what is simply new and unfamiliar. Unlike your child, you have had time to improve your skills at separating the potentially dangerous from the exciting but relatively safe. For your child, many more of his experiences are new, while as adults, we have frequently seen or done something similar in the past. From your perspective, a fearful response in your child may sometimes seem absurd, because your child is reacting to something you know to be innocuous, like a walk in the woods. But from your child's perspective, this is completely unfamiliar territory and therefore potentially dangerous. Think back to when you were a kid and imagine venturing into a dark forest. How many of these fears were going through your mind?

bugs   bad guys   lightning   spiders

bears   wild dogs   bees   quick sand   getting lost

wolves   snakes   poison ivy

It's possible these things might harm us, but it doesn't happen often, and we can learn to manage the risk. There are also the completely imaginary and impossible fears, such as

the bogeyman   ghosts   aliens   dragons

evil witches   monsters

and tigers (in North America anyway!).

Children tend to rely on adults to inform them about dangers. They need adults to tell them whether they should proceed (and if so, what preparation they might need in order to do so safely) or whether they should avoid the situation altogether. Psychologists call this reality testing. We teach our children to do this when we insist that they check with us before doing anything new or anything they are uncertain of. Adults who rely on others in a healthy and constructive way also do reality testing, for example when they talk things over with a spouse or friend before trying something new or taking some other action.

Children often don't know the difference between reality and fantasy, and become very frightened by the things they imagine or see on TV and in movies. What is seen on the screen or in the mind can

seem very real to your child. For children, seeing
is believing! Your child might be afraid of a monster
under the bed or in the closet, or perhaps of what might
be found in the dark, scary basement. Many of us can recall
feeling afraid of exactly these things. In situations like these, your
child feels certain that some harm is about to come to her, while you
are equally certain this is not true. To date, there are no statistics any-
where on children being harmed by monsters. (In a movie from a few

years ago, *Monsters, Inc.*, children discovered at long last that monsters have not caused anyone any harm, and thus they no longer believed in monsters. This was not good for the monster business!)

Sometimes children are anxious about things that have only a limited possibility of causing harm, things that are mildly stressful or uncomfortable, such as getting a needle in a doctor's office, going to a birthday party, or using a public washroom. Their response may seem exaggerated and out of proportion to the potential harm. You might expect that relying on you would solve this dilemma, and sometimes it does. Many children will ask, "Is it okay? Can I do it? Is it safe?" and, having received the okay, they will carry on with confidence. However your child may not be able to respond to your reassuring words, which can leave you as a parent feeling quite exasperated and worried about whether your child's anxiety is normal.

Perhaps, like many parents, you feel that you are powerless to subdue your child's anxiety, and that somehow this is your fault. You might assume that your child doesn't trust you enough to accept your advice, and this might leave you feeling frustrated or even hurt or angry. In some instances, there may indeed be a lack of trust, but in the many families I have worked with, this is generally not the case. In my clinical practice, I typically see an adult eager to be helpful and a child eager to receive help from the parent, both signs of a healthy parent/child relationship. The body language between the two often suggests a close bond.

The answer to why your verbal and physical reassurance is ineffective lies more in the strength of your child's highly active creative imagination. Your child's ability to imagine and visualize a fearful event in gruesome detail makes it impossible for her to feel the impact of your words. The vividness of her mental imagery can be so compelling that your reassurance falls on deaf ears. More about this in Chapter 2, where we discuss the incredible power of the imagination.

What to expect and what to look for

FIRST AND FOREMOST, when deciding whether the expression of anxiety is normal or not, it is important to consider your child's age. Some anxieties are considered problematic after a certain age but not before, and some anxieties are not even possible until a certain degree of mental development has been achieved.

Children develop anxieties only when they are intellectually capable of having them. Here's a good example: research done about fifty years ago by Eleanor J. Gibson and Richard D. Walk showed that very young infants around the age of six months are not afraid of heights. They will crawl over a glass floor through which a drop of many feet is clearly visible. They are fearless because they don't have the depth perception to see the drop. We can't be afraid of what we don't see! This is called the "visual cliff" phenomenon. When children get a bit older they begin to respond with fear, because at that point in their development, the cliff is seen and sensibly avoided. In this instance, fear is a learned response, something acquired with age. Of course, as the child develops and matures, some of their fears, the irrational ones, are overcome, while others remain. We retain our fear of cliffs, for example, because having it protects us from falling. It's a rational and useful fear.

Developing certain fears is a normal part of childhood. Many children respond to reassurance and simply outgrow their anxieties. Two of the common anxieties reported by parents of very young children are stranger anxiety and separation anxiety. Let's look at both of these important examples, the typical age of their appearance and why each is regarded as a problem only after a specific age.

Stranger anxiety

AS A CHILD DEVELOPS, many normal and predictable fears emerge. For instance, between the age of six months and three years, many children exhibit a fear of strangers. Since infants are extremely dependent on their caregivers, it is useful for them to be able to identify and cling to the person who is their lifeline. But sometimes stranger anxiety persists past the age of three or four and can spiral to include situations such as birthday parties and athletic activities. This can certainly take the fun out of anyone's social life!

Why is it that many young children exhibit stranger anxiety, preferring to stay only with familiar adults, while children over the age of three do this less often? As thinking develops, a child becomes more capable of reasoning and thus may be able to better manage her fears. She has likely had some experience with strangers, remembers previous encounters with someone previously unknown to her, and now has the reasoning power to connect previous events with each other. When encountering a new person, perhaps a distant uncle or aunt, she can make use of her idea of family and is much more likely to accept him or her.

She is also likely to watch carefully how you, her parent, act towards this person and to take her cues from you. Your behaviour is likely to be very different if the person at the door is a friend, a salesperson or a police officer. Your child has been watching your behaviour for most of her life and storing it in her memory. Like most children, she probably pays more attention to your body language and tone of voice than to your words. She notices how tightly you are clutching her hand or whether you are urging her to be polite and say hello. Depending on how you behave, as well as how she remembers similar people, your child will decide whether to accept a new person or be wary of them.

The key is that your child, at this later stage in her life, now has the increased cognitive capability required to engage in this complex mental task of sizing up a new person. She can put all the pieces together, her own thoughts and experiences as well as your cues, and arrive at a reasonable conclusion. She may not always be right – none of us are – but her behaviour will be very different from the reflexive and immediate reaction of the one-year-old in response to all strangers.

Some children, however, persist in being fearful of strangers long past age three, and if you are witnessing this in your child, she may need your help to change this behaviour. She may even recognize that her reluctance to participate in a particular event makes no sense, but may be incapable of overriding the intensity of the fear. Because she believes what her imagination shows her about the feared activity, she focuses on avoiding it at any cost.

Separation anxiety

BEFORE THE AGE OF FOUR, many young children are afraid of being apart from a familiar person or of leaving the home. This is called separation anxiety. In general, this age group often resists change, preferring what is known over what is unfamiliar and strange. When forced into a new and unpredictable situation, such as going to school on the first day, or switching to a new school, a child will often cling to a familiar adult as a way of ensuring his safety. While a child may experience the first day of school as the worst day of his life, after a few days, a sense of familiarity often takes over, and he grows sufficiently accustomed to the people, the surroundings and the routine. The anxiety subsides and he saunters willingly into the classroom. However, if after four weeks or more, your child is still refusing to leave your side or insisting that you accompany him to the classroom and remain there, then it is time to take action and remedy the separation anxiety. Many of the ideas and suggestions in this book should help you successfully assist your child to overcome this kind of anxiety.

Mental ability and anxiety – what's the connection?

YOU MIGHT BE SURPRISED TO LEARN that the emergence of separation anxiety and the ability to overcome it, as well as the readiness to begin formal education are all linked. This not a coincidence. All three are determined by the emergence of certain cognitive capacities which occur normally at this stage of development. In fact, the starting age for formal education is just about universal. That is, children all over the world begin school at roughly the same time, around the age of four or five. Our society and most societies around the world have come to the same conclusion, that at the age of four or five, children are cognitively, emotionally and behaviourally ready to engage in the challenge of school. School begins for children when they are, on average, ready for it.

At around four or five years of age, most children are capable of sustained periods of attention and of having reasonable control over their behaviour and emotions. Furthermore, at this age, a child is capable of engaging in productive and constructive learning, which includes meeting the expectations in a classroom, where a teacher's attention must be shared with many other children and where a strict routine is enforced. As well, at this stage of development, the child is able to function independently, at least for short periods of time.

If formal schooling begins too early, let's say at age three, teachers spend too much time trying to keep order and drying away tears caused by frequent conflicts and disappointments. Witness a recent *ABC Eyewitness News* report that the number of suspensions in preschool and nursery schools has risen over 200% in the U.S. over the past few years! It is not difficult to understand why. For many two- and three-year-olds, even though their cognitive development is proceeding normally, they are incapable of consistently behaving in the manner that would be expected in a school environment. Many children don't have the self-discipline required to sit quietly in a circle, pay attention to an adult reading a story, or even engage in reciprocal play with another child, share or wait their turn. Allowances need to be made for them, and they should not be punished because their cognitive development is not in sync with a school's unrealistic expectations.

Just as the changes in thinking capacity make it possible for your child to tell friend from foe and to manage the demands of a formal school program, anxieties are only possible when your child is able to envisage frightening ideas and possibilities. You may be tempted to believe that there is something wrong with your child's reasoning ability because his actions are so irrational. The truth is that the strength of his creative imagination can overpower his logic. As the imagination develops, so does the ability to visualize many kinds of images and sequences of events. This can lead to positive emotional reactions, such as joyful anticipation or excitement, but in some cases, the reaction is one of anxiety and fear. It all depends on which direction the imagination takes!

Enter the imagination

BEGINNING AROUND THE AGE OF TWO, your child's mental and creative capacities are enjoying a monumental growth spurt. Your child is now beginning to understand the connection between cause and effect, and he is better able to reason and use memory skills. He is also developing an imagination, the ability to conjure up all kinds of possibilities, real and fanciful. He is beginning to understand the concept of the future, or at least the immediate future, such as later today or tomorrow. Few children at this age are thinking about next year or even next month. In order to think about some time other than now, a person must be able to imagine what might be happening at that time. This could be something probable, highly improbable or even impossible. For instance, all of us can imagine the sun coming up tomorrow or ourselves getting out of bed, both highly probable events. We can also imagine aliens landing in Times Square tomorrow, although this is much less probable.

More on the power and importance of the imagination in Chapter 2, but for now it's important to know that anxiety and the imagination make their appearance at the same point in your child's life. Children differ with respect to the rate at which they develop milestone skills such as walking and talking, and the same is true for the emergence of the imagination. Many children develop a sense of imagination and a creative inner mind by the age of two, while for some it may emerge a bit later. It's not really important at what age it occurs; what is important is that anxiety and imagination arrive together.

From your vantage point as a parent, it is usually obvious when the creative imagination begins to emerge. You begin to see signs. You might witness your child's eagerness to flex her imagination in a number of different ways – drawing, making up stories or songs, creating imaginary worlds with dolls or action figures, etc. This is a joyful time for most parents, who are on the whole delighted and amused by their child's creativity and imagination.

It's at this point, however, that anxiety can rear its ugly head, because the imagination, especially in this early stage, isn't rooted in reality. Your child can and will imagine all sorts of things that could never possibly exist, like monsters or ghosts. She might also imagine things that are actually likely to happen but see them with much more intensity or magnitude than is realistic. The more vivid and developed your child's imagination, the more anxious your child may become. Anxious children, as well, tend to think more about the future than more relaxed children because their minds are filled with more imaginative possibilities. While an active imagination can lead to many hours of exciting and joyful play, it can also lead to frightening visual images and debilitating anxious states.

For example, I treated a young girl, Emma, aged five, who was terrified of the toilet. Even the sound of someone else flushing made her flee the room. She believed that she would fall in and be carried down the pipes, never to be seen again. Now it may be possible, es-

pecially if you are young and very small, to fall in the toilet
bowl and get a part of your body a bit wet, but it is impossible
for you to be carried away and down the drain. If your child is afraid
of the toilet, the image of the water sucking her down the drain may
be exactly what's occurring in her mind. For the same reason, some
children are afraid of the vacuum cleaner. I knew one child who was
afraid of escalators. She would view the step disappearing under the
floor at the top of the escalator and think, "If I don't jump off in time,
I'll get pulled down into the floor and disappear too." For a five-year-
old, that's quite a nightmare!

How can I tell what's normal?

ONE OF THE MOST COMMON QUESTIONS parents ask me is whether their child's fear is normal or abnormal. When asking this question, they are usually reacting to the tenacity and intensity of their child's anxiety response. They may have had repeated experiences of their child hiding under the bed when it's time to go to school or to a swimming lesson, or talking in a rapid, non-stop manner days before a planned sleepover in an effort to convince them to cancel the event or make other arrangements so they can avoid participating. These can be upsetting behaviours for a parent to observe, and it's hard to know what to do. You are right to ask whether this is normal.

Fear *is* normal and necessary. It is part of our biological and neurological make-up. All of us experience it, and, we would all agree, it is not something that anyone wants to eradicate. If there were a magic pill that could eliminate the fear response, it would be dangerous to put it on the market. In the absence of fear, people would make many wrong choices and put themselves in harm's way much too often. This is not a worthwhile goal!

Many of the fears expressed by children with anxiety issues are also expressed by adults and other children who might be described as better adjusted with respect to anxiety. Who isn't afraid of a large barking dog? Who isn't afraid of illness? Who likes vomiting? Who wouldn't be afraid of standing up and being criticized in front of a group of strangers? Many of the things feared by anxious children are potentially very harmful, even life-threatening. Dogs can attack; illness can be fatal. You might seriously question the good sense of a person who claimed not to have any fear of these things. Perhaps such a person might have taken that magic pill I referred to earlier. The fact that many of our children's fears have a basis in reality can make the decision about "normalcy" even harder to make.

Brave people experience fear and anxiety too! Many people who are viewed by society as exceedingly brave, such as firefighters and police officers, who put themselves in harm's way in the ordinary course of their day, often acknowledge that they experience fear – and not just in small doses. This fact is surprising to many people. It is a common misconception that brave people do not experience fear. In fact, I have noticed that when children are asked to define words on a standard IQ test, the most common definition given for the word "brave" is "not afraid." This is given full credit according to the official scoring criteria, but it is actually inaccurate. By their own accounts, brave people experience fear, often intensely, even while behaving courageously, but they simply don't allow their fear to control their behaviour.

In an interview on *60 Minutes* in 1979, Katherine Hepburn reported that she suffered from such debilitating performance anxiety that before every opening night performance on Broadway, she would vomit. She learned to anticipate this response, get it over with and then proceed with the performance. Even this extreme reaction did not prevent her from performing. The show must go on! Ms. Hepburn and other brave people do whatever is called for in the situation, in spite of the fear. The firefighter enters the burning building; the police officer chases the man with the gun; the ordinary person on the street acts courageously to save someone from danger. All of these people feel fear in their bellies, their chests or their throats, and yet act with courage, determination and bravery. Bravery is not the absence of fear. As John Wayne once said, "Courage is being scared to death and saddling up anyway!"

The price of anxiety

WHILE FIREFIGHTERS AND POLICE OFFICERS HAVE LEARNED to overcome their rational fears so they can go about their work, we don't all need to be heroes. But for some, anxiety and unnecessary fear make it impossible to lead even an ordinary life. In my experience, the characteristic determining whether someone has an anxiety problem or is functioning within the realm of normalcy is the *extent* to which the anxiety interferes with their life. If your child is worrying so much that he takes hours to get to sleep, refuses to eat in restaurants or attend birthday parties, or does poorly on tests in spite of adequately understanding the material beforehand, then worry and anxiety are interfering with having a normal, enjoyable and productive life. When your efforts to calm your child are ineffective and the behaviour persists over several months, then the anxiety needs to be reduced in both intensity and frequency, so that normal life can proceed.

When my clients are faced with the difficult decision of whether their child's anxiety is a problem needing professional attention or whether it's something they will eventually overcome, I often advise them to try to look as objectively as possible at how much of normal life is being sacrificed or put on hold because of anxiety. This is an extremely important assessment to make and one that will require some important decisions. If your child expresses a lot of anxiety, gives long explanations about things they fear, but then, with your encouragement, marshals the courage to take action, your child is definitely *not* suffering from an anxiety disorder. Your child, if she is behaving in this way, is likely to be an imaginative, articulate and intelligent person, who is aware of all the things that might cause harm, but is still managing to participate in the activities of her choice.

Many children experience significant amounts of anxiety, but are able to manage their feelings and not let their apprehension stop them from pursuing their desired activity. Evan, for example, was very nervous about going to overnight camp. He was having bad dreams and sleepless nights in the weeks leading up to departure day. The intensity of his feelings was so great that he woke his parents in the middle of the night for several consecutive nights to talk with them about his worries. When the time came, however, to leave for camp, he said good-bye, abruptly turned away and off he went. Once he was there, his parents received only good news reports from him and the camp personnel. In Evan's case, the anxiety was intense, but the outcome positive. The anxiety did not prevent him from going to camp or from having fun once he arrived. In the words of the British novelist and journalist Arthur Koestler, "Courage is never to let your actions be influenced by your fears."

If your child does not allow all the frightening possibilities to dictate his behaviour, then bravo! Your child deserves a round of applause for having courage and good judgement. The intensity of the anxiety reaction is not the defining factor, and neither is the length of time the anxiety persists. Your child might express worry and concern about an upcoming event for many weeks or even months, but then move forward and deal effectively with the object of his fear. Some people, like Evan, anticipate a lot more problems than are likely to occur, but they deal successfully with all their anxiety beforehand, leaving them relatively free of anxiety at the time of the event. This can be a very successful coping strategy, which psychologists call preparatory anxiety. If, however, anxiety is interfering with normal activity (e.g. cancelling camp, losing the deposit, having to be leave camp prematurely because of anxiety issues) and if occurrences like these persist, then this presents a different and more problematic scenario.

To help decide if your child has an anxiety problem, try answering the following questions:

1. Have most children outgrown the anxiety by your child's current age? If you have limited experience with other children besides your own, speak to a pediatrician, teachers, camp directors, sports coaches, experienced parents and others who interact with many children.
2. Does your child miss out on many potentially enriching and fun-filled events that she might enjoy because of anxiety?
3. Do other members of your family miss out on many desired events because one of your children is too anxious to participate?
4. Does anxiety prevent your child from participating in an academic, athletic or extra-curricular activity?
5. Does anxiety cause your child to perform poorly in an activity?
6. Does your child spend excessive amounts of time arguing with you and trying to convince you to change plans, so that he can avoid something that should be fun or worthwhile?
7. Do you feel that anxiety is determining too many of your child's decisions?

If the answer to many of these questions is *yes*, then this is a situation calling out for change. The ideas and techniques offered in this book will help you in supporting your child to take control of his imagination and manage anxiety better.

Key points to remember

✩ As much as parents would like to believe otherwise, childhood is not a worry-free and carefree time in life.

✩ There's a difference between fear and anxiety, although both are unpleasant emotions. Fear is a response to actual or threatened danger. Anxiety is a response to an imagined threat or to a threat that is exaggerated and out of proportion to reality.

✩ Children normally have many more fears and anxieties than adults. Many of these fears are outgrown as the person matures and has more experience with the world. Children often can't determine the difference between reality and fantasy because their experience with reality is more limited than an adult's.

✩ Children overcome certain fears, such as fear of strangers or fear of separation, when their thinking has developed to the point where they understand reality better. Sometimes children acquire fears when their development enables them to appreciate real danger, such as a high cliff.

✩ Children with a highly developed imagination are more prone to anxiety reactions because they are able to imagine many more frightening possibilities and imagine them with much detail and intensity.

✩ A certain amount of anxiety is normal, but when it dampens a person's enthusiasm for the regular activities of life and when too much of normal life is being avoided in order to silence the anxiety, then your child is in trouble and needs some help.

Chapter 2

Enter the imagination

TODAY, COGNITIVE BEHAVIOURAL THERAPY (or CBT) is the treatment of choice for many psychological problems such as anxiety and depression. It's an effective approach used to help adults make positive changes in their lives, and it's based on an understanding of the strong connection between thoughts, feelings and behaviour.

This chapter explores the difference between the adult mind and the child mind, especially the imagination. What is the role of the imagination, how is it related to anxiety, and what is its impact on our mind, body and emotions?

CBT teaches that in an adult, negative feelings, such as anxiety, sadness or discouragement, are the result of negative thoughts that fill the mind. CBT helps people change the content and quality of these thoughts and so allows them to break free from old behaviour patterns. Changing a person's internal message from "I'm a loser and I'm never going to amount to much" to "I made a mistake and next time I'll do better" causes negative feelings of despair and discouragement to be replaced with more positive ones, such as contentment and hope. This approach is used both in a traditional psychological framework and in a New Age, spiritual approach. You can find many self-help books which convey the message that when we are in control of our minds, we are in control of our lives. But notice that I've been talking about adults. There seems to be some difficulty in attempting to teach

this skill to children. The reason for this is that what happens in a child's mind is very different from what happens in an adult's. Simply put, children don't think like adults.

The visual life of children

FOR STARTERS, children think less in words and more in pictures and in visual images than do adults. As well, children are more action-oriented than adults. It is a rare child who will sit in a family session at our centre, passively and quietly waiting and listening, while adults chatter on about problems to be solved.

Most people will agree that children have more imaginative capacity than do adults, perhaps because they lack the inhibition of adults. In fact, this imaginative capacity is typically more vivid than in an adult, and it is largely defined by thinking in pictures and actions. While I very rarely see children who can give a clear, sequential description of a family situation, a great many children in my practice are able to recount every scene and action of a favourite movie. Their retelling of the movie is long and detailed, as if what happened in the movie is recorded on a virtual DVD in their brains and is being replayed for them internally as they describe it to me.

I have also noticed, after working with so many children, that they generally pay far more attention to their visual experience than they do to what is being said around them. Children watch and see much more than they listen and hear. They often pay little attention to all that we say, partly because adults say too much and use language that is too complex and abstract for them to understand.

The imagination of a child is adept at visualizing possibilities, and when those are negative, the impact can be brutal. A small fear is amplified in elaborate detail, causing the child to experience that fear with greater and greater intensity. The child is not simply afraid of germs, but he or she may see, in the mind's eye, millions of tiny germs attacking the defenceless body. An older child, say around age ten, might imagine herself in the hospital with tubes protruding from all orifices, the family gathered around with worried expressions on their faces, crying or asking, "Is she going to die?" while the poor patient lies there, clutching her stomach and gasping for air. A five-year-old might see herself becoming very weak, falling to the ground, perhaps being rushed to the hospital in an ambulance with sirens wailing, and being separated from her parent. Such a scene can be replayed a thousand times over in your child's mind!

The movies in our minds

RECALL THE LAST TIME you watched an engaging movie. Without noticing it, you got swept up into the story, so much so that you may have actually experienced "gut" reactions, as if the situation on film were really happening. If you saw a scene with a roller coaster on super speed, you may have felt a bit nauseated. If you saw the central character chased by an evil guy, you may have felt fear. Your heart may have pounded, your stomach may have been clenched, you may have reached out to grab something or someone. You may even have screamed. It was not happening to you, but it sure felt like it! And perhaps you stayed right inside the action until the lights came back on.

Children can get caught up in this sort of experience much more readily than adults, perhaps partly because they have less experience with what is truly real, and partly because they imagine events in more graphic detail. On a Saturday afternoon, looking around a movie theatre filled with children, you would actually witness many of the children jumping out of their seats or raising their arms protectively in reaction to something happening on the screen.

It is the vivid, often visual detail within a child's imaginary world that can seem as real to children as does the real world in which they live. Children, less able to differentiate between reality and fantasy

than adults, are the central characters in the movies they create. Talk about gripping intensity! Their bodies go through all of the physiological reactions they would if the events were happening in real life. The movies created by their minds are not constrained by reality, because anything and everything can happen in their imaginations. Their minds race like a runaway train. The results can frighten a child so badly that

he can become physically sick and not know where to turn. After all, how can you escape your own mind and imagination?

It is crucial to acknowledge the vividness of a child's imaginative process if we are going to understand how that imagination affects the way the child feels and behaves, and how it can cause heightened anxiety, stomach aches, panic attacks and all of the symptoms that parents often witness.

So let's say I'm a child who is afraid of going to school, afraid of what might happen there. If I am a creative and imaginative child my fear is not simple – I create an elaborate and detailed movie in my head. I might imagine not one child, not five, but the whole school calling me names. I might picture the entire class laughing at me for a wrong answer, a bad test mark or my awkwardness at sports. I see the same scene, or variations, over and over and over. I hear every word, every taunt hurled at me. It's torture!

This movie, unlike the ones we experience in theatres, lasts much longer than two hours. This movie extends over days, and I keep adding to the scenario. And what could be more interesting and captivating to me than a movie in which I am the main character, the star? It's no wonder I keep on watching my movie over and over again!

Why do we have an imagination?

THE IMAGINATION DOESN'T JUST PLAY A NEGATIVE ROLE in our lives, however. It enables us to play with possibilities, prepare for our future and escape from unpleasant realities. It is an important and enjoyable part of our minds. When we are children, we prepare to become adults someday by acting out different roles as we have observed and imagined them. One day I'm a storekeeper, another day a nurse, a teacher, a police officer, and so on. I remember once picking up my stepdaughter Sarah at daycare and finding her engaged in play with several other kids. They were playing "Bank." Sarah had arranged all the other kids lined up in front of a teller, and when one little one finally reached the front of the line, the teller in pigtails said, "No, you're in the wrong line! You have to go over there." This is what Sarah had observed many times in the bank and, to prepare for the future, she had the children rehearse this scenario exactly as she had observed it.

The wonder of the imagination is that it can be used to prepare us for the real world or for flights of fancy, for plausible situations or ones that are unlikely to be found in the real world. As children, we make up imaginary friends, and we believe in other characters such as Santa Claus, Mickey Mouse or Barney. Though purely creations of the mind, they become very real to us when we are very young.

At its best, our imagination offers us pleasure and joy. It allows us to conjure up whatever experiences we want, experiences which may be more positive than the challenges and disappointments we face in the real world. But for some children, what happens in their imagination isn't always under their control.

Helping your child deal with imaginary fears

AS PARENTS, we generally want to encourage our children to have a good imagination. I have never met a parent who hasn't been hugely proud of his or her child's imagination. Most adults are too busy with the daily grind of earning a living and taking care of the family to spend much time in creative pursuits. How many grown ups do you know who have time to spin a tale or compose a song, just for the fun of it? Sadly, not many. It is children, who, by and large, spend as much time as they can in this realm – that's what play is all about. As a parent, even if *you* have no time to play, you likely try to make time for your children to engage in this important activity. And you probably experience great joy in watching your child unfurl his storytelling or artistic masterpieces. Many a refrigerator is decorated with the products of children's creative impulses. It doesn't take much prodding for a mom or dad to share their praises for their child's creations or imaginative play. And they are right to be so enthusiastic; not all children are blessed with a vivid imagination or even a sense of play.

> "A good imagination is good, too much imagination … that can be really awful," a very anxious six-year-old, quoted in *Freeing Your Child from Anxiety* by Tamar E. Chansky.

But we need to be mindful that, for some children, a vivid imagination left unchecked can cause severe physical and emotional distress.

"I just turned my imagination around!" exclaimed a ten-year-old battling with his fears, reported by K. Young in a workshop on using a narrative approach with anxious children.

Therefore we need to teach our children to tame the imagination. Just as children are taught to master the body and its functions, so we need to help them be managers of their minds. Children who have the gift of creative imagination can, with the right attitude and tools, gain command of this inner power. The imagination can learn to follow the child's direction rather than tormenting him. But how can this be done?

My purpose in writing this book is to deepen your understanding of what your child may be experiencing and why, and to provide insights and tools you can use to help your child become the master of his or her mind. Here are some suggestions in two key areas.

Talk less and do more

AT OUR CENTRE, where we treat hundreds of families a year, we don't just talk to children. Of course we do some talking, but we don't *just* talk. Since children pay more attention to what adults do and much less to what adults say, we *do* something. We move around. We go over to the blackboard and write or draw something that is kid friendly, something simple and concrete that they can understand and relate to. We might draw a simple picture and say, "Here's a picture of your body. Come here and colour in how much of you feels sad. Colour in how much of you feels worried or scared." In this way, we address the fact that children's minds are oriented to seeing and doing.

In the past, we found that most children had difficulty maintaining their attention when the adults were engaged in discussions during family sessions. The well-behaved kids would typically sit and stare blankly into space, while the more active ones found something in the room to generate some action – turning over a garbage can, climbing on a chair, bothering a sibling. It was only when we stopped just talking and started to *do* something, that the kids decided we deserved their attention. Finally, they had a chance to understand what the session was all about!

Nowadays, we always have a basket of activities available – simple things such as crayons, markers and other concrete activities – so that while the adults are talking, the kids have something to do to keep themselves occupied. I believe that most kids actually listen better while engaged in some simple activity. Since we introduced that practice, everyone seems to be a lot happier in our sessions. You might consider doing the same thing at home. When traveling or planning to be somewhere for a lengthy period of time, like standing in a line-up or visiting a home where there are no other children, bring materials and activities to keep the kids occupied. You will likely have to contend with much less misbehaviour.

Help children refocus on what is real

MANY PARENTS FIND THEMSELVES going to great lengths to allay their children's fears. To prove to the child that there is no monster or ghost, they may wind up walking all over the house, opening all the closet doors and peeking under all the beds. At worst, this procedure just reinforces the child's belief that his or her fear is based in reality. After all, if you the parent are searching this carefully, the ghost or monster must be real! At best, it proves nothing: the clever ghost may still be hiding, and you just didn't know where to look!

Instead, one effective approach is to refocus your child in the right direction by demonstrating through your tone of voice and body language that you are not disturbed by the notion of a ghost or monster. Treat the object of their fear as exactly what it is – a product of the imagination. Suggest that you are intrigued and even pleased with how imaginative your child is. If you treat the object of their fear as imaginary, then your child will understand it as such.

Try saying something like, "Wow! What a wonderful imagination! Let's get out the markers and you can show me what the ghost looks like." Or another time you might suggest making up a story about the ghost or trying to get the child to fill in more imaginative details. Is it a boy or girl ghost? What does the ghost do for fun? Does it like scaring people? Be curious about this imaginative creation and ask all sorts of questions, just as you might take an interest in a piece of artwork or a castle made of sticks. The idea is to show your child that she has control over the image of the ghost just as she does over any other product of her imagination.

What if your child is worried or scared about something that is grounded in reality, at least in part? What if he is worried about other children being mean, excluding him from the group, calling him names? We have to admit that these things happen; they happened to many of us when we were children. When your child is recounting these events, several things are occurring simultaneously. To begin with, it likely brings back images from your own past of all the times similar things happened to you. What is critical is that you try to help your child separate truth from fantasy. In your child's mind, the experience he is having is likely to be a mixture of both. In his mind, the scene is probably more elaborate than what actually happened, especially if he has a good imagination. Imaginations like to embellish the truth.

You might say to your child, "Pretend I'm you and you are them. Tell me what they said. Show me what they did." In all the assessments I have done – and I've now completed thousands – one of the questions I ask repeatedly is, "Are you bullied, picked on, or teased much?" Kids often answer, "Yes." Then I ask, "What do they tease you about?" And the responses are often innocuous, such as "They make fun of my name. They call me Tommy Bommy" or "They make fun of my shoes 'cause they're blue." In fact it is often the jeering tone of voice that hurts the most, rather than the actual words that are spoken.

At its best, our imagination offers us pleasure and joy

I am well aware that serious incidents of bullying – including physical assault – do occur, and I am the first to call the school and move into action if this is necessary. I also am aware that girls can do as much harm as boys, if not more, with relentless verbal abuse and exclusionary tactics. These instances, however, are the exception rather than the norm. Nevertheless, when our children talk about "other kids being mean and not letting them play," our *own* imagination can be thrown into high gear and we envision the worst. We need to keep our own fears in check so that we can refocus our children on the reality of the situation and find a way to help them turn things around.

Key points to remember

☆ Imagination is usually associated with fantasy. When asked about the imagination, most people talk about Disney cartoons or other Hollywood movies. But think of yourself waiting in a doctor's examination room, looking at all the sharp instruments, picturing how they might be used on you. That's the imagination at work, too!

☆ It's important to remember that children have more active and vivid imaginations than do adults. Children are much more involved in their visual sense than are adults and often think to themselves in pictures more than in words. They play-act different roles, draw pictures and move their dolls and action figures around to demonstrate a story line. Knowing this allows you to engage your child in exploring their imagination and ultimately gaining control of it. Given the power of the imagination, we had best start calling the shots!

Chapter 3

The mind fills a vacuum

IMAGINE BEING A YOUNG CHILD and discovering your inner life. With this new self-awareness comes the realization that sometimes your mind has a mind of its own! Your mind gets going on something, and, if you don't know there's an off-switch, you simply have to follow wherever it leads you.

The creative mind doesn't like to be bored; it loves to be entertained. And what's more entertaining than a movie in which you are the main character? If that movie turns scary, however, anxiety can be the result. The remedy is learning to discipline your mind.

As a kid, I used to have lots of guilty thoughts. I would worry for days about something mean I did to another child. Or suppose my mom asked me if I had broken that teacup she found in pieces on the kitchen floor. I might lie and say, "No." Well, that lie would play over and over in my mind. I'd wonder if and when Mom would find out I had lied and what consequences lay in store for me.

If by chance an adult had been observing me at this time, they probably wouldn't have noticed anything out of the ordinary. They would have seen an outwardly calm child, perhaps slightly subdued. Part of me continued to engage in whatever activity I was involved in, playing with dolls or doing jigsaw puzzles. But a good part of my internal life was focused on replaying the lie and worrying what was going to happen once my lie was discovered. Needless to say, while I was caught in this guilty spiral, I wasn't having much fun.

As parents, we teach our children to care for themselves in many different ways. One early lesson is how to eat properly, chew food well, and select a variety of nourishing foods. We teach them to care for their bodies, to clean themselves properly, and to treat an open wound so as to avoid infection. We teach them about the importance of sleep, so they have energy for the day's activities. Although all these things are vitally important, human beings are more than just bodies in space. We also have minds, and an important part of learning to care for ourselves is finding out how to manage our minds. For many of us, this is difficult, simply because no one ever taught us how. Of course we've all learned a trick or two over the years, but how can we teach our children if we're not even aware of what we do? Because I've made the study of the mind my life's work, I will share with you what I've learned and explain how I teach it to the children I see in my practice.

The childlike nature of the mind

THERE'S A COMMON CRY I hear from parents: "I don't know what to do with her. She has a mind of her own!" It certainly is a challenge to deal with someone else's mind, but even dealing with your own mind presents problems! I explain to my clients that your own mind has a mind of its own, and what's more, it often goes off in a different direction than you would choose. In many ways, our minds and our children really do share many similar features. Because children have minds of their own, they often behave wilfully or become cantankerous just at the worst moment. You may have plans, but your child seems to have very different ideas. He might choose to be upset about a forgotten item of clothing and refuse to get on the airplane, just as they announce that it's boarding time. Or he might have a meltdown in the car, when the weather and traffic are both demanding your full attention.

What makes children stir up trouble at times like these, "for no apparent reason," as parents so often tell me? If you observe children, you'll notice that they won't tolerate monotony for long. If they are not actively engaged in something, they clamour for our attention and will even misbehave in order to fill up the empty space. I believe that for most children, when nothing much is happening, the emptiness is almost intolerable. It's better to get everybody riled up and see how it will turn out, than have too much peace, quiet and nothingness. This is also true of the mind. If there's too much empty space, the mind goes looking for trouble.

Suppose you decide you want to sit down to read a book or do some work. All of a sudden your mind wants to think about anything but that. What your mind comes up with is often much more captivating than balancing your chequebook or reading the manual on how to work the DVD player. Before you know it, you've dropped whatever you were doing, because you weren't really concentrating on it anyway. Your mind has succeeded in distracting you once again. Why does the mind do that? Why won't it just let us do what we set out to do? The simple answer is that we haven't trained it to be compliant with our wishes. Just as children need to learn to control their impulses and comply with the expectations of others, your mind, too, needs to learn to be disciplined, which means it needs to learn to listen to you.

One of the main reasons why your mind won't listen to you is that, just like a child, your mind does not like to be bored. Let's face it, balancing a chequebook and reading a manual are not the most exciting activities. So when presented with a boring or a repetitive task, the mind creates a more interesting scenario for its own entertainment. It's quite peculiar, however, that the mind does not seem content to focus on something pleasant for very long. You might abandon balan-

cing the chequebook and choose to sit outside in the backyard, but if you don't give the mind something interesting to focus on, it is likely to latch onto something unpleasant – the bees that have been visiting your backyard, or the ongoing struggle you're having with your neighbour over the proposed fence, for example.

Have you ever wondered why your mind seems to dwell on the negative? This is a question that psychologists have been grappling with for some time, and so far, there is no agreed-upon answer. It may be that our brains are hard wired to protect us from danger, that we have evolved this way in order to survive. It seems to me, however, that one important part of the answer is that intrigue and drama are just plain interesting. They relieve the boredom of everyday life, and that's why the mind seeks them out.

It's much more amusing to think about the possibility that some-one might be lurking in the basement than to think about how nice the sky looks. You might admire the patterns of clouds in the sky for a few fleeting moments, but it's not something that is likely to linger in your mind for an extended period of time. Thoughts about the possibility of your losing your job, however, or of someone being mad at you could occupy your thinking and keep you entertained for much of the day. Or you might dwell on some physical symptoms you are experiencing and wonder if you are coming down with a cold or even developing a serious illness. The possibilities are truly endless. The thoughts that distract us typically involve some element of danger, excitement, in-trigue or suspense.

The cinema of the mind

IN FACT, IF YOU WANT TO KNOW what kinds of things the mind finds entertaining, think about the movies that become real blockbusters. How many of us would stick with a movie about a contented person living a simple, happy life? If the scenery were particularly stunning we might stay with it for a few minutes, but after commenting, "That's pretty!" we would probably leave the theatre because nothing much was happening. In fact, nature scenes are often used to relax us and put us to sleep. The movies that pull in big audiences typically involve danger, excitement, intrigue, suspense and tragedy. Interestingly, these are the same scenarios the mind will create on its own.

One way to look at this is that the movies we flock to see are sim-ply extensions of the movies that are constantly playing in our minds, but taken to an extreme degree. We relate to what is happening on the screen because we have similar experiences in our own lives. We have danger in our lives, although we don't usually have someone trying to kill us. In our daily lives, danger might take the shape of trouble at work – "Will the boss fire me for that mistake I made?" – or financial problems – "How is my tax audit going to turn out?" When we see a movie on the screen, we identify with the character on the screen: we imagine how we would feel in his situation. We come away feeling that, no matter what kind of trouble we are facing in our own lives, it's not as bad as it is for the guy we just saw on screen. And besides, the two hours we just spent involved in someone else's life gave us a brief escape from our own internal movie.

Of course, the movies which our minds create are of special interest to us. After all, it's happening to Me, not to a stranger or to a fictional character! It's real, isn't it? Well, a lot of what we experience as real is actually not as real as we might think. Our minds are capable of embellishing the truth and creating many scenarios that are possible but unlikely to actually happen. For example…

One day you go to work and find that your co-worker has been laid off. Immediately your mind is propelled into action, creating intrigue. You wonder, "Will I be laid off too?" You might start by recalling all the conversations you've had with your boss about your productivity or lack of it in the last while. There may have been a few comments that you review in your mind, replaying them over and over, looking for clues to whether you might be next on the list to lose your job. Your mind might then start thinking about what would happen to you if you were laid off – lapses on your rent or mortgage payments, your car payments, other bills going unpaid. Before you know it, in your mind, you are homeless and guilt-ridden, having let down your family. This internal movie is both suspenseful and tragic. Poor you! Poor everyone who knows you and depends on you! What a sad tale!

The reality may well be that you won't lose your job, and that your boss is not even considering firing you. But you have just spent the last hour or maybe more locked in a movie in which not only are you laid off, but you and your family have become outcasts from society, homeless and destitute. The more details you include and the bigger the supporting cast, the more interesting the movie becomes: *The Story*

of Poor Me. Of course, as the movie unfolds, you become increasingly upset. How can you possibly do any work when this kind of movie is being played in your mind? Whew! This is all too stressful! Recall, however, that you haven't actually been fired, and that it may never happen. Furthermore, the time lost "watching" this "movie" can never be reclaimed.

Getting control of the mind

I LEARNED A LOT ABOUT THE MIND from meditation, which I have now been actively practicing for over thirty years. I still recall the very first time I tried to meditate. I sat in a circle with some of my friends and was told by the leader to close my eyes and focus on my breathing. I felt self-conscious and silly closing my eyes, focusing on myself and ignoring the other people in the group. I opened my eyes many times to see what others were doing: were they actually following these directions or simply sitting there and staring at me? After I realized that others were trying to follow the instructions, I began to try it myself. That's when my mind began playing tricks on me.

As I tried to focus on my breathing, which is pretty boring, my mind generated a lot of excitement to lure me away from such a dull activity. My first thought was that I had forgotten to lock my car, and I started to imagine my car being stolen. I was able to resist the impulse to check my car, but then I had another thought. Had I turned off the oven at home? I had visions of my rented home going up in flames. I wanted to jump in my car and drive home, but again I resisted the impulse. Needless to say, I did not experience the inner peace reflected on the face of Buddha. In fact, I would characterize what was occurring in my mind as nightmarish. With all the horrors I was imagining, I could barely keep myself seated for the required fifteen minute session.

What I know now that I didn't know then is that I was experiencing the impact of an undisciplined mind. My mind had not yet learned how to take instruction from me and how to focus on what it was directed to focus on. My mind was still operating on the principle that its sole purpose was to find entertainment and to avoid boredom.

Very few of us have ever had any training or direct instruction on how to contain our thoughts and fantasies. It may seem like a daunting task. One mother, sitting in my office at our first meeting, looked at me with a perplexed expression when I told her that her son needed to learn to have some control over his thinking. She said, "I didn't even know that was possible!" Where do you even begin training of that kind?

Disciplining the mind is not as difficult as you might think, but it does take some persistence. Training your mind is a lot like teaching a young child to behave. Think about what happens when a child of two is continually drawn to play with an electrical outlet or something else in the house that is forbidden. How would you teach him? You might start by finding clever ways to block his access. If that's not possible, you would repeatedly tell him, "No, don't touch that!" and actively refocus his attention on something else. You would take away what he is being drawn towards and distract him with an alternative.

This method also works to train and discipline the mind. Say "No" in a gentle but firm way and give your mind something else to focus on. However, it's not good enough simply to say, "No, don't think about spiders," or whatever it is that's worrying you. You need to go one step further. As we've seen already, if there's a vacuum, a hole with nothing in it, the mind will fill it quickly with a different but equally scary, nightmarish thought. But if you say, "No, I don't want you thinking about losing your job. I want you to think about the menu for Friday's dinner party instead," then your mind will go in a more constructive, pleasanter direction.

Sometimes our efforts to redirect our thought don't work the first time, and we need to try again. You might choose to focus on something you enjoyed, like your last vacation. But that might generate a thought such as "I won't have any more vacations when I lose my job." Then, just as you would continually and patiently redirect your two-year-old away from the outlet, you need to keep redirecting your mind away from horrific visions of a future with no vacations. You keep redirecting your mind and giving it something interesting but pleasant to think about until your mind learns that you are in the driver's seat and that it will go where you tell it to go, not the other way round.

Helping the child discipline the mind

ADULTS, EVEN THOSE WHO HAVE NEVER BEEN DIRECTLY TAUGHT to refocus their minds, have probably found ways to make this process work for them. Perhaps you have found that when your mind insists on thinking negative and frightening things, you get busy with cleaning the house or baking a cake. Or you might call a friend, read a good book, or do something on the computer. As adults, we have many ways of distracting ourselves from our inner thoughts. Children however, especially the highly imaginative and creative children for whom this book is being written, have had far less experience with avoiding the frightening thoughts and images created by their minds.

Why is it especially important for an anxious child to learn to discipline the mind? Learning to manage the mind is an important part of being human, but unfortunately, babies don't come with instruction manuals, and so we all learn how to be human the hard way, from experience. Children who suffer from anxiety need to learn this skill sooner rather than later because of the special gift they have been given. As we saw in Chapter 2, with an exceptionally good imagination, the mind will generate vivid internal movies which may seem even more true to life than life itself. The sometimes wicked and nightmarish scenarios they envision can leave children living in a kind of hell, until they change it. It's like buying a ticket for a horror movie when you were expecting something else. You might feel glued to your seat until it's over, not realizing you could end the nightmare by just getting up and leaving the theatre.

Children are sometimes convinced that going along with their imaginations is a good thing, and so they resist changing the practice. They have not learned that sometimes going along with the imagination is a good thing and sometimes it's unwise. They need our help to become more discerning. Of course, by the time they become adults, they will have discovered many of the strategies that you have learned and maybe a few more. But if we help them now, we not only save them years of misery, but we also give them the opportunity to be the masters of their minds and to begin using their energies more constructively and at an earlier stage.

In some ways, the children I work with seem to latch on to the idea of being in charge of their minds more readily than do adults. Children are already focused on developing control in so many areas of their existence. They are learning to control their bodies, to master bicycles,

roller blades, jump ropes, soccer balls and baseballs, hockey pucks and sticks. Also, they are acquiring intellectual skills, learning to read, do math, etc. Childhood is about achieving mastery and control over a host of different objects and activities, so it fits into the paradigm of childhood to become master of the mind. In my experience, many children rise willingly to this challenge once it is explained to them.

It is helpful if a child has had some experience taming or learning to control something else, like a pet. A new puppy needs to be encouraged, through a lot of repetition, to stay off the couch or bed, not to chew up the furniture and to relieve himself only outdoors. His behaviour needs to be curbed or refocused. This is the same process that needs to occur with respect to training the mind.

If the child has no experience with pets, I talk about learning to ride a bike and using training wheels. In the beginning, when we are just learning to ride, we fall often. The training wheels help to keep us upright until we learn to balance. We simply keep trying until our bodies and minds make the connection.

There's another way in which learning to ride a bike is like training the mind. For both our bikes and our minds, we have to learn to
use the brakes and to steer properly. For both, we need to be able to
go in the right direction, to say, "Stop! Don't go there. Go over there
instead!" And we never stop steering or using the brakes. The bike
can't steer or stop itself! No, we need to stay awake and alert, steering
and braking as long as we are riding. We have to do the same for our
minds. Controlling the mind is a lifelong skill.

Giving in to fear strengthens the fear

AS WE SAW IN THE PREVIOUS CHAPTER, many anxious children spend
a lot of time in the worlds created by their imagination. Their imaginative capacity is often more highly developed than that of calmer children. What is a parent to do when a child becomes completely caught
up in frightening images created by his imagination?

As a parent, you may see your child screaming and shivering with
fright, carrying on as if something horrible is about to happen. You
probably feel helpless because you see nothing, and your reassuring
words fall on deaf ears. It may seem too cruel to force your child to
sleep alone when he is certain there's a monster under the bed, so you
give in and let him sleep with you. The physical comfort of having you
close seems to quiet him. Besides, you'd like to get some sleep yourself. Giving physical comfort and reassurance is the easiest and most
expedient thing to do.

However, giving in to fear in this way strengthens the fear and also
reinforces the idea that the way to lessen the fear response is to run
away from the imaginary object and stay close to someone. Doing this,
however, will increase the clingy behaviour that is so often associated
with anxiety.

As we saw in Chapter 2, these children have the gift of a vivid
imagination and firmly believe that what they imagine is real. The
solution, then, is to teach them to distinguish what is real, what is
imaginary, and what is possible but highly improbable. We can start
by treating the unreal and imaginary as such. When children imagine

monsters or ghosts, we need to demonstrate our firm belief that these are fabrications of the mind, not realities. Giving in to the behaviour and allowing the child to sleep in a parent's bedroom or fall asleep on the couch leads the child to conclude that there must be a good reason for all this abnormal change in routine, a good reason to be afraid. Remember, it's not what we say but what we do that communicates the most to children. Refer back to Chapter 2 for other appropriate ways of coping with imaginary fears.

Key points to remember

☆ All of us, particularly children, have a tendency to let our minds wander, and a wandering mind will soon get itself in trouble! By the time we are grown up, most of us have picked up a few techniques for distracting ourselves from unpleasant thoughts, but children can be taught directly how to guide their minds.

☆ The trick is to recognize an imaginary scenario for what it is – just imaginary – and to give your mind something more constructive to focus on. This is especially important for highly imaginative children because it can save them years of anxiety.

Chapter 4

The future tense

MANY ANXIOUS CHILDREN tend to think too much about the future. They are always imagining all the terrible things that might happen and they have too little experience to properly evaluate what is likely to happen and what is unlikely. We need to give our children tools for evaluating what is real, what is likely and what is unlikely. We all take risks. We gather information from credible sources, we take precautions and we venture forward. And this is what we want to teach our children: to be able to plan sensibly for the future without being trapped in a cycle of worry.

As we saw in the last chapter, anxiety is connected to our ability to imagine the future. However, anxiety is also an adaptive function, allowing us to plan for undesirable situations and deal effectively with them. Here, I will discuss how we can teach our kids this important life skill.

With all this discussion about the awful places our minds can take us to, we are likely to forget that there's a purpose to all of the things our minds create. Even anxiety has a useful purpose. Where would we be if we couldn't imagine the future? We'd be stuck in the present and only able to respond to events as they unfolded, with little preparedness. Imagining the future enables us to make elaborate plans and hopefully to avoid much unpleasantness.

This ability to think about the future works in many ways. We plan for both the immediate future and the long term. We think about what

we need for later today, tomorrow, next week, next year; some of us even think about many years from now. If we do this in logical and reasonable ways, this is an asset. Of course one can over-prepare, spend too much time thinking about an event, and then have little time left for actually living and experiencing the moment. Carly Simon wrote a song many years ago called "Anticipation," in which she warned about the dangers of thinking too much about the future:

> We can never know about the days to come
> But we think about them anyway
> And I wonder if I'm really with you now
> Or just chasing after some finer day.

In contrast, there are some people who live for the most part from day to day, hardly ever thinking about the future. There are both advantages and disadvantages to this way of being in the world. Living in the moment allows a person to be more in touch with his or her sensory experience and hence have a stronger sense of being alive. Many of us experience this sense of aliveness when we are playing an action sport, such as tennis or basketball, where we are rewarded for being in the moment and penalized if we're not. For instance, if you think too much about the future or the past when playing an action sport and stop focusing on whatever is happening in the present moment, then you might miss the ball or the puck that is coming at you *right now!* Most of us enjoy these experiences of being in the moment, and we seek them out. Sports activity is one of the healthier ways of staying in the present, but there are other forms of excitement that require us to be alert. Some of these are high risk activities like skiing, driving at high speeds, and even engaging in criminal behaviour. All of these require that we be on our toes at all times, which makes us feel more alive.

Children generally think less about the past or the future than do adults. They are typically more engaged in whatever is currently happening. This is one of the aspects of childhood that adults often envy. Because young children are not typically thinking about possible consequences of their behaviour, they are naturally more spontaneous and less inhibited. When something excites them they squeal with delight! They don't stop to think, "What might happen if I squeal? What will others think?" They simply experience the joy of the moment and squeal! When children play with each other, or even by themselves, they give free rein to whatever impulses emerge. Whether it's rough-and-tumble play or chatter-and-pretend, they play without thinking too much about it. Time does not exist for them in these states. Oh, how we envy that!

But at some point, we change. For some of us this happens at a younger age than for others. Our minds and imaginations develop to the point where they begin to dominate our experience of ourselves and of life itself. In a young and imaginative child with excellent mental capacity, the mind begins to create what I like to call the *what if's*. Because the mind has the ability to think about all kinds of possibilities, it does just that. Because your child's mind may also be one of those that creates a highly detailed visual experience, your child may not only think about many different possibilities, but may embellish them with lots of vivid details. So now, instead of squealing with delight, she may think about all the people in the room, how they will might respond to her squeals. She might remember the last time she squealed and what people did or said, replaying those scenes over and over in her mind. She might even expand on the instant replays and imagine people storming out in disgust, or casting dirty looks in her direction, or other kids saying things like "I'm not going to play with you anymore or be your friend!" So, instead of being in the moment, she is standing there with a blank look on her face, imagining the past and the future. What's going on in her mind is indeed very interesting, but it is all imaginary: it's happening in her mind but not in reality. She is missing the present moment and is not engaged in what's actually transpiring in real life. Eckhart Tolle in his book, *The Power of Now*, speaks plainly when he says, "The future is usually imagined as either better or worse than the present. If it is worse, it creates anxiety. [But] both [the past and the future] are illusory."

What I have observed many times over is that children who suffer from anxiety seem to get stuck in the *what if's* to a much greater extent than children who do not have a problem with anxiety. The list of *what if's* that these children rattle off to their parents and to me in sessions is truly remarkable. Their parents and I often sit in amazement and awe at the degree to which they have thought something through, working out all the possibilities that might occur in a particular situation. After hearing their child give twenty or more reasons why they should not attend a particular event or do something that most people consider safe and enjoyable, a parent often gives up in defeat. Generally parents can come up with good reasons why *some* of those horrible things are not going to happen, but they usually get stumped by at least one. I know many children who are terrified of germs. It's hard to prove that even if you wash and sanitize, there's not one germ hiding somewhere or to prove to a child that a lurking germ will not cause harm to someone.

The only way out of this dilemma is to focus on the cause of the problem, which is not the germs but the child's mind, which has taken off and is out of control. Like adults, children must learn to avoid dangerous situations or to take action to remedy them, and then to stop worrying about the things they can't control. For example, even people who live in California don't think about earthquakes every day, although an earthquake is a very real possibility in that part of the world. What good does it do to worry about it? Absolutely none at all! North American engineers do a pretty good job of making buildings and bridges as earthquake-proof as possible. Witness the minimal damage caused by recent California earthquakes compared to the damage caused by earthquakes elsewhere. Simply worrying about earthquakes did not make people safer. However, doing something to prevent damage made a lot of people safer.

How to help children turn off the what if's

TO BEGIN WITH, children need to know that we all have *what if's* in our minds, that generating *what if's* is what the mind does. Recall Chapters 2 and 3, where we discussed how minds like to be entertained. The *what if's* are a great source of entertainment. By the time we become adults, we have imagined millions of those *what if's* and almost none of them have become realities. Through that process many adults have learned to dismiss many of the *what if's* as the hogwash that they truly are. They have learned not to become too wrapped up in their own fantasies, not to go down those roads to nowhere. Children have not yet learned this. But we can at least let them know that we used to do the same thing, that we've learned not to do it, and that life is a lot easier when we don't do it.

I know many children who worry frantically as soon as an adult is late coming home. In their mind's eye they imagine that their parent has been in a traffic accident or has been kidnapped by a "bad guy." I recall having many of those frightening thoughts as a child. But even though I was consumed by terrifying fantasies hundreds of times, never once did any of those fantasies turn into reality. Eventually, I began to understand the truth of the saying "Bad news travels fast." I realized that if something really bad happens, you'll find out about it soon enough, and so I stopped anticipating disasters.

One way to learn about reality is to simply live with it long enough to learn how it works. The other way is to be taught early that we have these feisty, creative and cantankerous minds, which need to be reeled in. Some children don't want to learn from the experience of adults. They insist on learning things the hard way, from their *own* experience. But even these children can be helped. We can give them tools for controlling the mind, even when it turns into a runaway train, as so often happens.

Strategies for controlling the mind

ONE WAY TO HAVE SOME CONTROL over the mind is to write things down, and in particular to rate things on a scale – say, from 1 to 10. So you pull out a piece of paper and you ask the child to write down all the bad things that will happen if he does … whatever is worrying him. Or if the child is very young, you offer to do the writing for him.

This may seem so simple, but writing things down accomplishes many things. First of all, what may have appeared to be an infinite list, all of a sudden becomes a very finite list. It may have seemed as if there were a hundred reasons not to go to the birthday party, but now it appears that there may be only seven or eight. Ask the child to rate each one on a scale of 1 to 10, with 10 being the scariest. This also is a way of exerting some control over the experience. Now it seems that only two of the reasons are very scary and the rest maybe less so.

Next, you enter a problem-solving mode with your child and figure out what you really want to do and can do about the situation. After you deal as well as you can with the reality of the situation, then you and your child need to talk about how she can put some constraints on her creative mind and steer it in a different direction. This usually involves acknowledging that it has gone wildly off track and then giving it something else to focus on. Here are some great ideas from kids I've worked with:

☆ Thinking about something creative and engaging, like a circus with animals doing interesting tricks.

☆ Using their creative imaginations and imagining putting the scary thoughts inside a balloon or bubble and letting it go off into the universe, far away from them.

☆ Writing down the scary thoughts on a piece of paper and putting it in a box and putting the box away somewhere in the house for safe keeping. If the child is too young for writing thoughts in words, then have him draw pictures of the scary ideas and images.

Chapter 5

Sweet dreams are made of this...

IF YOU CAN TEACH YOUR CHILD good sleep habits, you will be giving him a gift for life. The process of falling asleep is very much a learned habit, and like many other learned habits such as training your body to go to the bathroom at convenient times, it requires repetition, and lots of it. In teaching or learning this habit, it is also important to recognize the paradoxical nature of sleep. Getting to sleep does not respond well to direct effort. The more you try to go to sleep, the more sleep eludes you. In fact, trying hard actually wakes you up. So the last thing you want to tell your child is "Go to your room and just try to go to sleep." This will likely lead to more frustration and more wakefulness.

Ah, if it were only that simple. For some kids, especially after an invigorating day that has included some intense and exhausting physical exercise, sleep comes as soon as the head hits the pillow and the lights are out in the room. But, for many kids, getting to sleep is like a nightmare that starts even before they are asleep. In this chapter, I am going to share with you everything I've learned over the years about sleep and how to help kids get to sleep.

Why can't my child get to sleep?

CHILDREN WITH BUSY MINDS often have trouble getting to sleep. And if you have an untamed mind that is used to doing exactly as it wants

to do, why should it all of a sudden obey the command to be quiet and allow sleep to overtake you? The answer is… there is no good reason why it should and often it just doesn't. As you have already learned in this book, it is imperative, especially when you have an incredibly busy and active mind, that you establish who is really in charge – you or your mind.

When someone lies down and closes her eyes, this is precisely the time when the activity of the mind accelerates. All of a sudden the action of life stops, and there are no external distractions. Because there is nothing interesting to focus on, the mind becomes bored. It then begins creating thoughts and images, and the more active the imagination, the more creative the productions of the mind. A busy mind will start generating worst-case scenarios, such as "Oh my god! What if I didn't do my homework correctly? What if I did the wrong homework?" Or, higher up on the intensity scale – "What if I get left out of playing with my friends again?" or "What if so-and-so is mean to me?" Or, even higher up – "What if that noise I just heard means there's a robber in the house?" If you have a vivid imagination, then you are not simply mouthing these words. No, each of these thoughts comes complete with an internal movie and lots of vivid imagery, enough to elevate anyone's heart rate. Clearly these are not the right conditions for drifting off to sleep.

Reminder: You are not your busy imagination!

WHEN YOU PUT YOUR CHILD TO BED you are not simply putting his body in the bed. You also need to put his mind to rest. A good way to do this is to develop your own special bedtime dialogue, which you

use every night as part of your child's goodnight ritual. The goal is to make it a habit, something that, when done over and over in the same way, generates the same outcome – the desired outcome.

What should this dialogue include? The routine for putting the mind to rest involves first telling the mind that it is being put to rest. Then there is a review of the day, both good and bad. Then you might touch on some good things to look forward to the next day. If there are any troubling issues or concerns that the child brings up or that you know of, you might mention them and, with the help of the imagination, put them somewhere special for safekeeping. That special somewhere might be an imaginary vase or a colourful box where these problems go until the time is right for dealing with them. You can tell your child that there's no point thinking about them now because nothing can be done about them now. And anyway, late at night is not when we do our best thinking.

Then, depending on the child's age, you might go through a list of all the good and cherished things in her life, all the people who love her and whom she loves in return. You can mention all the wonderful things she has, such as a nice room, a nice bed or lots of stuffed animals, and all the good things she has to look forward to. As you drift off to sleep it is more pleasant to have lots of positive thoughts in your head.

Some sample dialogues for putting the mind to sleep

"WE'VE COME TO THE END of another wonderful day, and it's time to put your mind and thoughts to rest. What were the good things that happened today? Any things that weren't so good? That's okay. Life is made up of good and bad. We can learn from the bad things. It makes us stronger and wiser. Is there anything we need to put in the box for safekeeping? We can get to it later when it's the right time. If thoughts about those things come back, gently say, 'Not now. Go back in the box. I'll get to you later.' And now let's list all the people (and pets) who love you. And now say good night to this day because it is done. Tomorrow will be a new day, but now it is time to let it go and be at rest."

Sometimes it is necessary to do a bit more to help a child learn to relax and turn off the mind. Here are a few ideas:

You might suggest to your child, "Breathe in deep, deep down, the way a baby breathes. Allow the breath to come in and go way down inside you. Just relax and let your belly rise and fall, rise and fall." You might put your hand gently on your child's belly so that your hand rises up as the belly expands. If you do this, give your child soft, positive feedback as the belly expands. Say, "Yes, very good, that's it." Many children try too hard to get this right. If your child's efforts seem laboured, simply say, "Let the breath do all the work. All you need to do is feel the breath come in and out and watch your belly rise and fall."

With older children you might say something like "Breathing is a miraculous thing. Every day, thousands of time every day, your breath takes what it needs from the air, the oxygen, and brings it to your body to use for energy. Every inhale brings the oxygen to you. Every exhale gets rid of what your body doesn't need anymore – the carbon dioxide. You can use this miracle to take in other things you need and get rid

of what you don't need. You might breathe
in fun, success at school, lots of friends, or
scoring goals. And on the exhale, imagine
all the things you don't want or need, like
sadness, or upset, or worry. Just let them
go and take a free ride out of your body
on the exhale. Let it go! You don't need it."
Do this as long as the child wants to. It is fun imagining all the things you want coming into you and all
the things you don't want going out of you into the world at large
and being carried off. They can go off in a hot air balloon or whatever
comes to mind.

Another useful strategy is to give your child a peaceful scene to
focus on as he drifts off to sleep. Remember that the mind doesn't like
being told to think of nothing. If the screen is blank, the mind is likely
to fill it with something it finds interesting, which means it will be
scary, or suspenseful or action-oriented, which often wakes the child
up. If you try this strategy it is helpful to use the same restful scene
each time. Once it becomes a habit, then all the child will need to do is
put himself in that scene and off to sleep he will go. Here are a couple
of examples:

"Imagine you are lying on a cloud, and the cloud is drifting ever
so slightly from one side to another and slowly moving down towards
the ground. You are nice and comfy on this puffy cloud, drifting from
side to side and enjoying the swaying motion of the cloud as the gentle
breeze brings you down and down into the land of slumber."

"Imagine you're on a raft on a lake and the gentle waves are moving the raft from one side to another, and you sink deep and deeper
into the raft and smell the water beneath you. Feel yourself swaying
and drifting from side to side and slowly moving closer to the land of
slumber."

I have taught this next one to children as young as eight. "Imagine
you are standing in front of a blackboard or a whiteboard. You have
a piece of chalk or a marker, and an eraser. Now imagine you pick
up the chalk. Feel it in your fingers. Feel the smoothness against your

skin. Perhaps it feels cool to the touch. Reach up your hand and slowly draw the number one. You might start at the top, or you might start at the bottom, or you might even start in the middle. It doesn't matter. Wherever you start is the right place to start. Feel the movement of your hand and arm as you write the number one. Completely draw the number one. When you are finished, put the chalk down. Now pick up the eraser and begin to erase the number one. You might start at the top, or the bottom or you might even start in the middle. Wherever you begin is the exactly the right place to be. Erase every bit of the number one. Feel the movement of your arm as it erases. Take your time. When you are finished put the eraser down. Now pick up the chalk and write the word S-L-E-E-P. You might print it or you might use your cursive writing. Either is fine. Write every letter and feel your arm, enjoy the movement of your arm, as you write the word S-L-E-E-P. Take your time. When you are done, put down the chalk and pick up the eraser and begin to erase the word S-L-E-E-P…" Continue in the same pattern with the number two and so on until the child is asleep. Few people get past the number six.

This exercise is a good one because it is a positive experience yet fairly boring and repetitive – just the right conditions for inducing sleep. It is also a bit more interesting than simply counting sheep. It involves several senses – sight, touch, smell – and gentle movement as well. And finally, it incorporates the suggestion of sleep.

Sometimes you have to trick your mind

AS I SAID IN THE BEGINNING OF THIS CHAPTER, you cannot force yourself to sleep. In fact, direct effort often produces the exact opposite of what is desired – more wakefulness and often frustration and anxiety along with it. So, as the French philosopher Maurice Merleau-Ponty said, "When we go to sleep, we lie in bed and imitate a sleeping person and hope that sleep is drawn to us." What can we do if sleep does not come as soon as we would like? If you give yourself a harsh scolding and tell yourself you must go to sleep, sleep is unlikely to come. If you imagine being up all night, tossing and turning and being miserable, if you think about what's going to happen the next day after you have been up all night, if you spend time thinking about unpleasant things, then for sure sleep won't come. But sometimes you can trick sleep into coming by saying, "It's okay. I can lie here and not sleep and still be okay and then sleep might just come."

What if it's your child who can't sleep, even after you've gone through the soothing bedtime routines described in the previous section? In this situation, you can suggest to your child that he will be just fine if he simply lies still for a while and thinks to himself about all the good things that were said during your bedtime dialogue. Instead of fretting about sleep, he might say to himself, "Even if I can't sleep, it's okay. I have lots of pleasant and nice things to think about. I am cozy, warm and safe in my bed and I can just lie here thinking about all those nice things." Eventually sleep will come.

The science of sleep

IF YOU OR YOUR CHILD ARE HAVING TROUBLE GETTING TO SLEEP, you might be interested in what science can teach us about sleep. Here is some of what I have learned:

Scientists have identified four different kinds of brain waves that move in different patterns during the twenty-four hours of the day. But if you are trying to help your child understand how the brain works, it's best to simplify. Since children tend to think visually, the image of a wave rising and falling is a good representation of how the brain cycles between sleeping and waking. You can explain that sometimes we are more awake and sometimes we are drowsy and closer to sleep. When you are very much awake, you can picture yourself at the top of the wave, the point where it is more difficult to get to sleep.

Adults and children alike cycle through varying phases of alertness. Even when we are asleep, sometimes we are deeply asleep, and sometimes we are closer to a more awake state. If you have fallen asleep and then suddenly find yourself awake, as many children do, then your waking brain waves are on the rise and it is more difficult to turn them around and get yourself back to sleep. If you are in a deep sleep and then something awakens you, it is usually quite easy to fall back to sleep because even though your eyes are open you are basically still asleep. If you try to get back to sleep when you are essentially wide awake and your brain waves are moving towards more wakefulness, then you are working against nature. It would be like trying to turn a bike around when it is heading straight downhill. It can be done, but it requires braking, getting off the bike and basically changing direction.

It's a lot simpler to let yourself go down to the bottom of the hill. Then sometimes the momentum of going down can propel you half way up the other side. So, if you or your child wakes up in the middle of the night, do something like reading a not-too-exciting book or listening to some music for about twenty minutes and then go back to sleep. Why twenty minutes? Because it takes about twenty to thirty minutes to move from the awake to the drowsy part of the brain wave cycle. Why fight nature when we can work with it? If it's time to go to sleep and you or your child finds that drowsiness seems far away, then read or listen to music until drowsiness sets in. It will come.

Key points to remember

☆ Just remember that when your child is getting out of bed and complaining that she can't get to sleep, it is because her mind has not been put to rest.

☆ Just as you are having trouble with your child, so she is having difficulty controlling her own mind.

☆ When you put your child to sleep, don't just put her body to bed. Help her put her mind to rest and she won't be jumping out of bed so often.

Chapter 6

Putting it all together

HOW DO YOU GO ABOUT CHANGING how your child looks at the problem of anxiety? It's not as difficult as you might think. When I see a child in my practice, I get to know the child and discover what she's interested in and what things she has already learned to control. As the parent, you already know those things. In fact, you are an expert on the subject of your child, so you're ahead of the game.

STEP ONE – *Let your child know that his imagination is an amazing gift!*

Not all children are blessed with such powerful and creative imaginations. Let your child know he has an amazing gift! But both you and your child already know this is true. With a vivid and active imagination, every day, every event can be a joyful experience. If your child has any doubt about this fact, I'm sure you can offer many specific examples from his daily life.

We've come to the chapter where we put it all together. Here you will find six steps towards helping your child to overcome anxiety. You will learn how to help your child make the connection between anxiety and the gift of imagination and recognize that the imagination can be controlled in much the same way that a person learns to master any difficult skill. By the last step, your child will be well on the way to taking charge of the problem and achieving a solution that will make a significant difference in his or her life, now and in the future.

STEP TWO – *Imaginations sometimes go off on their own, and so control is needed*

Explain how the imagination can either work for you or against you. Sometimes the imagination seems to have a mind of its own, and it takes paths that cause us lots of anxiety and fear. When that happens we have to take charge.

Here is part of a transcript of a conversation I had with an eight-year-old girl who had an extreme fear of dogs.

THERAPIST: [Looking at child.] Did you ever realize that there's a connection between your imagination and your anxiety? When it goes where you want it to go, it's a good thing. When you're playing with your dolls and you're making up stories, that's a good thing. But sometimes, your imagination goes where it wants to go, but not necessarily where you want it to go. And that's not such a good thing, is it?

CHILD: [Child nods her head in agreement.]

THERAPIST: When you hear a barking dog, what does your imagination do? What do you imagine that dog doing? Is he ferocious? Does he have big teeth?

CHILD: Yes, he's biting me hard and ripping open my leg.

THERAPIST: Wow! That's a pretty awful picture you've got there. Do you really want to keep that picture in your mind?

CHILD: No, not really.

STEP THREE – *Find examples of other difficult things your child has already learned to control*

Look for examples in your child's life of situations where she has learned to control something or has mastered a difficult skill, like riding a bike. Suggest to her that in a very similar way, she will be able to gain control over her imagination.

THERAPIST: Your imagination is something you need to learn to control! Did you know that?

CHILD: No, I didn't.

THERAPIST: Do you ride a bike? Did you learn to skate?

CHILD: Yes, I ride and I learned to skate backwards. I like to skate.

THERAPIST: Was it hard to learn those things, or easy?

CHILD: It was kinda hard. Skating backwards was *really* hard.

THERAPIST: Were you falling a lot? Riding a two-wheeler, was that hard? Do you remember?

CHILD: It was hard.

THERAPIST: But you did it. How did you do it?

CHILD: My Mommy left one training wheel on the bike.

THERAPIST: That's a new one. So you had one wheel you could lean on. [Therapist standing up and demonstrating leaning on the training wheel.] Imagine riding a bike, if you didn't have brakes or a way to steer. What would that be like?

CHILD: It would be hard!

THERAPIST: If you don't have brakes or steering, you can go out of control. Or if you hit a bump in the road or a rock, what would happen, if you didn't have a way to steer? [Pantomiming all of this.]

CHILD: I would fall off.

THERAPIST: Do you think you might even hurt yourself?

CHILD: Yeah, I could hurt myself.

THERAPIST: You learned how to control your bike by using the brakes and steering with the handlebars. You need to learn how to brake and to steer your imagination. Because you have a vivid imagination, you need to learn to control it.

STEP FOUR – *Exploring the inner movie*

Find out what is occurring in your child's inner movie when she is anxious about something. What is her actual inner experience? Ask action questions like: "What do you see?" "What are you doing?" "Who else is there?" "What are they doing?" "What happens next?" Ask as many questions as you can think of that will allow you to see the inner movie your child is witnessing and experiencing. Stay away from questions like "What are you feeling?" Or "Why are you feeling that way?"

THERAPIST: Well, when you make up stories with your dolls or imagine other stories, I wonder if you kind of see what's happening and see it pretty clearly. Is that right? Do you get pictures inside your head?

CHILD: Yes!

THERAPIST: That means you've got a really vivid imagination! When you see the dog biting you, the picture of that seems pretty real. It's just like it's really happening. That's why your body reacts and you get those panicky feelings. Your body doesn't always know the difference between what's real and what you're imagining. When we're dreaming, we think it's really happening. We wake up and go, "Whew! I'm glad that's not really happening." But your body reacts as if it's all real, and you get those panicky feelings. When your mind shows you that picture of a dog biting you, it's a really detailed picture because you

have such a vivid imagination! So your body thinks that
dog is really biting you. But is he?

CHILD: No.

THERAPIST: Is he biting you in your imagination?

CHILD: Yes!

STEP FIVE – *Making the connection between anxiety and the gift of imagination*

Here's the clincher, the part that seals the deal. With all of the enthusiasm and sincerity you can muster, tell your child that she has

an amazing gift, a wonderful gift of imagination, and that this is a truly fabulous thing. But because it is such a powerful gift, she needs to learn to tame it, to be in charge of it, so that it doesn't rule her life. With hand gestures and tone of voice conveying the importance of this message, lay it on thick.

THERAPIST: Your imagination is a Wonderful Gift! I don't want you to go away from here thinking that it's not a wonderful thing. Imaginations are precious. Not everyone has as good an imagination as you do. You are lucky! A lot of eight-year-old girls have already left their imaginations behind.

MOTHER: Not her!

THERAPIST: Because it's satisfying and she enjoys it. When she grows up, she will likely do something creative because she's a creative person. [Turning to child.] Right now you need to learn to be in charge of it. And it's not easy, just like learning to ride your bike is not easy. Learning to skate backwards isn't easy, but you can learn all of these things.

When your imagination is going down the wrong road, and it shows you a "movie" of a dog biting you, then you have to be able to say "No, I don't want to do that movie." You have to turn it in a different direction. Does that make sense?

You can't just say *No* to your imagination, because the imagination doesn't like to do nothing, just like kids. Kids don't like to do nothing – they say they're bored. You have to give your imagination something to do – something that you like.

Gifts can be wonderful if we learn how to be in charge of them, but not so wonderful if they're in charge of us. Sometimes the gift gets away with us.

How much of the time are you in charge of the gift? How much of the time are you in charge, and how much of the time is your imagination in charge and taking you to places where you don't want to go? [Therapist goes to board, draws line, asks child to show how often she thinks she is charge. She divides the line about 60/40, showing that she is in charge 60% of the time.] So it looks like you're in charge more than half the time, but your imagination is in charge quite a bit, about 40%. Is that right?

CHILD: Yep.

STEP SIX – *Put your child in charge*

THERAPIST: One of the things we have discovered that helps is to put one's worries in a box. [Looking at mother.] Adults do this when we say "I'm not going to think about that now, I'll think about it later." We call it "compartmentalizing." Well, kids need to *actually* do it, to put it in a *real* box.

We call it a worry box, and you can write her worries on paper and then put them in a box, or she can write or draw them. You can then take them out and even bring the box here to the Centre when you have sessions and look at what's in the box, to see if you want to talk about it then. But putting it in the box is like putting it away, so that you can go to sleep or do your work or whatever it is that you want to do, so that the worries don't get in the way of you doing those things. [Looking at child.] Would you like to do this?

CHILD: [Nods vigorously.]

Your attitude makes a difference

AS ANY CAREGIVER CAN TELL YOU, the job of raising children is so much more complex than anyone ever anticipates. Parents really are their child's first teacher and the person from whom their child learns the most. Parents teach their children to speak, to be toilet trained and to take care of their bodies. Not only do they teach physical skills like drawing, running, and throwing a ball, but they also teach where it's okay to do these things and where it's not acceptable. As well, parents must teach their children how to participate meaningfully in the culture in which they live, which includes some of the hardest lessons of all: manners, hygiene, social skills, moral values, and taking responsibility for one's actions. It really is endless! It's worth noting that most of this learning falls into the broader category of mastery or control of something.

But probably the most important area of all may also be the one least often taught directly: controlling the mind. If the cognitive psychologists are correct, and I think they are, then when you have your mind under control, you also have mastery of your behaviour and emotions. I think many parents may not even attempt to teach their children this important skill because no one ever taught it to them. Naturally they are sceptical about whether it can be learned and are at a loss even about how to begin. But I know from experience that it can be taught and learned. Many of the children I have worked with have proven to me that given some direction and encouragement, even very young children can master this skill with practice and add it to the repertoire of things they have mastered.

In helping your child to achieve this mastery, it is essential that you, as a parent, pay even more attention to what you do than what you say. Why? Because that's what your child is paying attention to! As we go about our daily routines, our children watch everything we do and emulate who we are. A recent study about the choices children make during play provides a good example of this. Children, aged two to six, whose parents were smokers and drinkers, were four times more likely to include pretend smoking and drinking in their play activities than children whose parents did not smoke or drink. Therefore it's essential for parents to be good role models. Just telling them to do something won't be effective if we model something else.

So if we want to help our children control their anxiety, we must first learn to control our own imaginations. Although we live in an age dominated by anxiety and by the threat of terrorism, we must practice putting our own demons to rest. We must evaluate every fear on its merits and realize that living one's life is a series of calculated risks. Let's be realistic about those risks. Take, for example, highway driving. All of us are aware of the risks involved, and yet I see very few children, except perhaps those who have been in serious car accidents, who are fearful of riding in cars. The reason for this is that most adults, even if a bit fearful of highway driving, still get in the car and drive. We know that driving is dangerous, but we take reasonable precautions and go about our business. In doing so, we provide good role models for our kids.

Another essential skill we teach our children is how to differentiate between what's real and what's imaginary, and how to focus on what's real. If your child says he was "bullied," find out what actually happened, scene by scene, action by action. Get the facts straight. Make sure you're not making the situation worse by imagining extra details yourself. If your child says he is afraid of something that you know to be imaginary, treat that fear as exactly what it is – a product of the imagination. Marvel at your child's creativity in coming up with something that interesting and unusual. If you give in to fear, the child notices that and concludes there must have been something worth giving in to.

As parents, our goal is to give our kids the tools they need to face life, not run from it, and modelling the right attitude ourselves is the way to start.

Key points to remember

When communicating with children, remember…

☆ Use concrete language – language that describes pictures, or things that you can see, touch and hear. Kids think concretely. If you use a word that you think they might not understand, explain it to them using a visual image.

☆ Make it fun and easy, because children lose interest quickly. Keep your language simple and to the point.

☆ Don't just use words; act out what you want to express. Use body language and big gestures. Think of other ways to communicate your ideas that will capture their attention. Less talk and more doing will keep a child's attention.

☆ Invite your child to communicate with you in a way he is comfortable with. If your child is not capable of explaining things in words, ask him to draw or even act out his fears.

Chapter 7

Give me tools and strategies!

WHEN PARENTS COME TO MY OFFICE with a chronically anxious child, they often express the hope that I can give their child specific tools and strategies for dealing with the problem. They often tell me that they have already offered their child many strategies, but since their suggestions have not worked, the parents think they must be on the wrong track. They seem to feel that their own creativity is lacking, that somehow the strategies coming from a psych-

A specific set of tools and strategies is exactly what many parents are looking for when they bring their anxious child to see a therapist. But wait – it's just not that simple. First you have to be sure that your child really is ready to make a change in his or her life. Once you are sure that your child is motivated, then you'll find the tools you need in this chapter.

ologist's office will be different, better, more effective. In many cases, this is far from the truth. Many of the strategies that parents offer their children are typically just as good as anything I might offer, but the problem is that the child is not motivated to use them.

This lack of motivation can be perplexing, especially since the anxious child is in distress. So, when a child is first brought to see me, one of the first things I try to explore is how motivated the child is to make things different. To get a child to explain his feelings, it's best not to ask in words alone. As we saw in Chapter 2, children think less in words and more in pictures and visual images. Therefore, to get a clear answer, it can be very helpful to formulate the question using a picture or a graph or a numbered scale. Many of the visual techniques I use with children come from the Solution-Focused approach developed by Insoo Kim Berg and Steve de Shazer, who founded the Brief Family Therapy Center in Wisconsin thirty years ago. Further work was done by Bill O'Hanlon, whose elaborations I find extremely useful in working with children.

Years ago, at the children's mental health centre where I still work, before we had adopted the Solution-Focused approach, we regularly found that our family interviews were disrupted by the children misbehaving while the adults chattered away. It was only in the 1990s, when we began using Solution-Focused tools like scales and circles, pictures and graphs, that the children really took notice of what the adults were doing. Nowadays, many children, as soon as they enter my office, make a beeline for the whiteboard on the easel and draw the scale. Typically, they love this intervention, because it gives them an opportunity to communicate what is most important to them without having to use a lot of words and complex sentences. When I ask them how they feel, they often stand thoughtfully in front of the whiteboard, pondering their answer for many minutes, trying hard to get it right.

This is an extremely powerful way of communicating with children about a myriad of different things. If you're concerned about a child's level of sadness, marking his mood on a scale is a very effective way to take his emotional temperature on a daily basis. How sad were you today? And what might we do to move you one or two points towards a more positive mood? Another

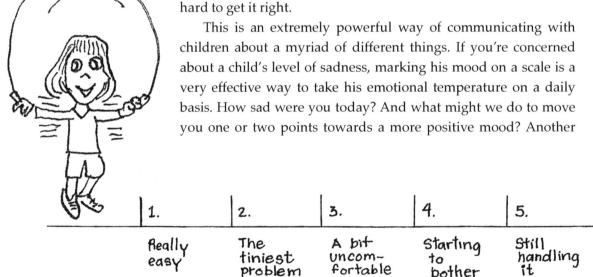

1.	2.	3.	4.	5.
Really easy	The tiniest problem	A bit uncomfortable	Starting to bother	Still handling it

similar strategy is to draw a large circle and ask the child to show how much of that circle shows his sadness, or his fears, and how much is left for happiness and fun. You can play around with it and divide the circle up any way you choose.

By the way, these strategies are not just for children. It is often difficult for many of us, adults included, to put our thoughts and feelings into words that convey the meaning accurately. With a scale or graph, however, we can show clearly the intensity of our distress or feeling. This technique is now often used in hospitals to ask patients about their level of pain and discomfort. Because of the clarity of the response, health professionals are able to provide better pain management.

In dealing with a child who has a problem with fear, for example, I might ask the child to rate the size of his problem on a scale from 1 to 10, with 10 being the biggest problem in the world, and 1 being just a little problem. Whatever they say I accept as truth, and then we talk about it. If they say it's a 10, then I might ask how it affects them in their life: what makes it a 10? If they say it's just a 5, which, by the way, is the response of many children, then I might ask, "How come it's only a 5?" Since the parent is also in the room, I usually ask the parent to rate the problem, too. This exercise often reveals to both parent and child that they have different estimates of the seriousness of the problem and different levels of motivation for change.

I remember one particular case in which a four-year-old girl had been sleeping in everyone's bed except her own. The family, which included two parents and two other siblings, was distressed and sleep deprived. In the interview, we drew the scale on the board and every-

6.	7.	8.	9.	10.
Getting tough	Pretty tough	Really tough	Starting to lose Control	PANIC! Make it stop!

TEXT FOR SCALE ADAPTED FROM AUREEN PINTO WAGNER'S FEELING THERMOMETER

one in the family rated how upset they were that the four-year-old was not sleeping in her own bed. After everyone finished, the therapist asked the four-year-old if she had known how everybody felt. The child looked shocked. She hadn't known, or if she had, she hadn't known it this clearly. Seeing everyone's feelings so clearly represented had a powerful impact on her. It provided sufficient motivation for her to change, and, from that moment, she slept in her own bed.

Once everyone in the family, including the child, has a clear idea of how motivated he is for change, we are ready to move on to the next stage. If your child is highly motivated and clearly wants to make changes, then by all means move ahead and introduce the idea of tools and strategies. If, however, there is a lack of motivation, then our first task is to create some desire for change.

One major reason why children may not be motivated to change is that anxiety comes with some benefits. As we saw in Chapter 3, the movies that children create in their minds are downright fascinating. The next time your child tells the tale of how she was afraid to walk into the public washroom, or was so fearful of entering a house with a dog, you might notice the big smile on her face as she recounts everything that happened, the great lengths she went to avoid whatever it was she feared, and how everyone around her responded to her fear. It's all very interesting and adds up to a very good story. Children don't usually convey this sentiment in so many words, but their facial expressions are communicating loud and clear: "Wait till you hear what happened next! Wow! It was amazing!"

Children need to understand that their creativity in this regard is misplaced. If they continue to get caught up in their own horror movies, they are likely to be to be hurt by their imaginations, rather than using their imaginations constructively and growing up to be creative, productive individuals. It can be very motivating to say to a child, "If you don't get control of this, it's going to control you and run your life. Is that what you want?" If they give the right answer, which is "No, I don't want that," then you are ready to move on by giving them the tools.

Another major reason children may not be motivated to change is what psychologists call secondary gain. This means that the anxiety symptoms and how others respond to them provide something positive in the child's life. For example, because a child is unable to sleep at night, he might sleep with a parent or a sibling, which can be a lot more fun than sleeping alone, at least for the child. Or, if a child is fearful of being alone and is unwilling to change, someone may stay home with him, and, as a result, he gets a lot more individual attention. Having that much control over events and over significant others can be a big plus from a child's point of view.

Many of the issues we have discussed in previous chapters can be used to motivate children to want to overcome their anxieties. In my conversations with my young clients, I encourage them to understand that if they don't develop adequate control over their powerful imaginations, they will never be truly in charge of themselves. Their minds will be running them for a very long time. Parents can frame the problem in the same way. This takes the power struggle out of the realm of parent vs. child. Instead of a conversation about what the parent is or is not doing to make the world risk-free, the struggle is now in its rightful place – it becomes a struggle between the child and some aspect of himself.

For all of these reasons, it pays to take the time to make sure that your child's motivation is strong and properly directed before trying to implement change. If you proceed too quickly and then it doesn't work, you might jump to the wrong conclusion, that the strategy or the tool was wrong, when in fact, lack of motivation and bad timing were the reasons for the failed outcome.

I know some of you are waiting very impatiently to receive those magical tools that are going to make all the difference in the world to your child, but there's one more point we have to discuss first. Most of the kids I have worked with, especially these very creative and anxious kids, are less interested in other people's strategies than in strategies they make up on their own. Of the hundreds of kids I have helped

You and your child will have many good ideas that will work just as well as the tools mentioned here. Feel free to adapt or change any of these tools to suit your needs or tastes. If you're willing to share your ideas, please contact me, so that your tools can be used by others. For information on how to get in touch, please visit my website at **www.docrobin.com**.

by now, I don't think that two of them have ever used exactly the same tools in getting to the end result. As I tell all the kids I see, every person on the planet is unique: no two snowflakes and no two people are exactly alike. So what works for one person is different from what might work for someone else.

For example, Jennifer, only seven years old, walked into my office with her mother, clutching a reprint of an article I wrote that had been recently published in a magazine. She could barely read, but she was bright and curious and wanted to know what the article said about anxiety being a "gift," an idea that was in the title. She was adorable, with long pigtails and bright blue eyes, but she had so much going on in her brain that her speech came out in a rapid-fire manner. Her words were also somewhat indistinct, so that neither I nor her mother could understand what she was trying to say. When her mother and I, working together, were able to slow down her speech and get her to communicate a bit more clearly, I was able to teach her about her mind and her imagination. I asked her if she wanted to do something about taking charge of herself. She looked at me with a serious and intent expression and said in a loud, clear voice, "Yes, I do." I believed her. I then asked her if she had any idea how she could do that. She said, "Of course! I'll send my mind a text message!" and she laughed with glee. Once again I had to admit that yet another child had invented a new method of gaining control, a method that both surprised and delighted me.

Rules of thumb about tools

MAKE SURE TOOLS ARE CONCRETE. This means they should be visible to the child and, if possible, incorporate things they can touch, see and even hear. Use drawing and writing as much as possible. If you're out in public and don't have paper and pencil, remember gesturing can do in a pinch. Hold your hands out and say, "How big is this feeling you're having? Is it this big?" (using your hands to show a small space) or "Is it

THIS BIG?" (moving your hands far apart to show a very large space). Remember, when we just use verbal communication, we are expecting that the child will be able to visualize in their heads everything we say. Not everything we say is amenable to that process, especially for children.

Remember to convey to your child the idea that whatever she is experiencing and feeling at any given moment is not where she needs to stay, and that there are things she can do to change her current state, condition or feeling. Sometimes things change on their own, sometimes someone else intervenes to make us feel better, and sometimes we can actually take charge and make change happen for ourselves!

Don't expect your child to remember everything that you discuss or draw or act out. Use cue cards and symbolic drawings and place them everywhere the child might see them and find them useful! Use Post-it notes! Use construction paper! Be creative!

The tool box

TOOL #1 – *A Feeling Body*

Draw an outline of a person, and ask your child to draw where feelings are in the body. You can ask him to colour in the body and show how intense different feelings are. You are asking him to identify where he experiences different feelings and to show how strong those feelings are. It is often very interesting to see what colours children associate with different feelings. At some other time, you might use this colour-code in your conversations. "You're having a blue day today. How can we redden it up a bit? How could we get more green in there?"

TOOL #2 – *Scales and Thermometers*

I have already mentioned this extremely useful tool. Simply write down numbers from 1 to 10 and identify one end of the scale as okay and the other end as a high level of distress. Here's an example:

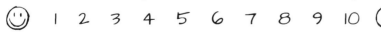

The happy and sad faces on either side give children an immediate visual understanding of the scale. In her book, *Worried No More* (2001),

Aureen Pinto Wagner has a "Feeling Thermometer" which includes a description of each number on the scale. Number 1 is a "Piece of Cake," number 5 is "Not too Good," and number 10 is "Out of Control! Ballistic!"

One important component of using scales is the discussion that can occur around the child's responses. If the child says he is at a particular level, the adult can ask if he is comfortable at that level. "Is this where you want to be?" If not, then, "Where would you prefer to be?" "What would feel okay?" "When was the last time you were at that comfortable level?" Just follow your own curiosity about what these numbers might mean for the child. Try not to move too quickly through all this. Your child will likely be enjoying and appreciating the fact that you are interested in where he is. You can make summarizing statements, such as "Let's see, you were at a 10 when such-and-such happened, and that hadn't happened in a very long time. Is that right? You don't like being at a 10. It feels awful. You wouldn't mind being at a 5. Is that right?" Then you can start to explore how to get from a 10 to a 5. What kinds of things might help the child to make that improvement? And if going from 10 to 5 is too big a jump, then how can he move from a 10 to a 9 or an 8?

I have used scales with children as young as three, and they have understood the concept surprisingly well, but if you feel this is too abstract or confusing for your child, you can use blocks. One block means he feels just a little bit scared, and a pile of ten blocks is up-to-the-sky scared.

TOOL #3 – *Lists, Lists, Lists!*

We all like lists – they make us feel better. Just knowing we've put it down leads us to believe that we are going to get to it, if not sooner, then for sure later. Anxious children typically have lots of lists in their heads, but usually they are lists that are more likely to create anxiety than quell it. So this list is for all the things that make your child feel better. Ask her to come up with her own title: "List of Happy Things" or "List of Things That Work" or "List of Things That Help." She can start with a few ideas that come off the top of her head. Perhaps you

can add a few suggestions, and then, as life experiences unfold, keep adding to the list. Every time you do something that works or your child does something that works, add it to the list. Post the list in a visible place in the child's room, so she can review it from time to time or refer to it when a crisis is occurring. For very young children, the list should have lots of pictures that portray the actions on the list. The picture can be drawn by the child or cut out of magazines.

TOOL #4 – *The Magic Triangle, the Baseball Diamond and the Tracks of My Tears*

The Triangle tool was first introduced by Philip C. Kendall of Temple University in his workbook for children *The Coping Cat* (1990). The diagram shows Thoughts, Feelings and Behaviour, each at one point of the triangle, but all connected by the triangle's sides. This tool

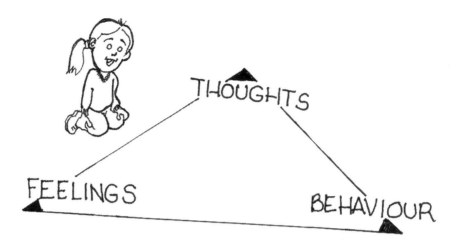

is used to generate a discussion which focuses on how thoughts create feelings and then result in behaviours or actions. A therapist I know has the triangle drawn in the middle of her office floor with coloured masking tape. The kids stand on each point of the triangle and say out loud what they are thinking, then what they are feeling, and then how they might be acting.

Robert D. Friedberg and Jessica M. McClure in their book *Clinical Practice of Cognitive Therapy with Children and Adolescents* (2002) expand this notion to a baseball diamond and to a train station. Drawing the diamond on a board, they identify the different bases as Thought Base, Feeling Base, Body Base (where you feel the feelings in your body), and then Action Base or home base.

The train station or Tracks of My Tears depicts different stations: Mind Station, Who Station, Where Station, Feeling Station, Body Station and lastly Action Station. The adult asks the child questions and fills in the information about what happens at these different stations. All of these are concrete tools to illustrate complex concepts and to communicate them to children.

TOOL #5 – *A Safe Place*

This is a tool often used by hypnotherapists for both adults and children, but you can use it without actually hypnotizing your child. Ask your child to create and experience a safe place, a place that is absolutely secure and comfortable. It can be indoors or outdoors, but, for children, it should not be their own room. Too many things occur in a child's room; it is often where he or she is sent for time out, and it is therefore associated with misbehaviour. A safe place can be somewhere the child has actually been, like a beach or a mountain top one may have visited on vacation, or it can be an imaginary place.

The idea is to flesh out all the details with the child. Many children will likely want to draw their ideal place rather than just experience it in their minds. You can guide them by asking certain questions, such as "What's the weather like? Is there a breeze? Is the sun shining?" "Are there flowers and plants? Is there water – a stream, a lake or an ocean?" "Is there a comfortable place to sit or lie down?" "What is around you? What do you see there?" If it's indoors, "What are the furnishings like? What's on the walls?" Once the child has created this safe place, then remind him that this place is always available. All the child needs to do is think about it and go there in the imagination.

TOOL #6 – *Just Because*

In an article written in 1991, James E. Elliott suggested the "Just Because Technique." Robert D. Friedberg and Jessica M. McClure also discuss this technique, calling it a verbal means to "debunk the myth that opinion means fact." This is an excellent technique for very verbal children, those who believe in the power of words. It goes like this: you insert the words "just because" before a automatic negative thought and at the end, change the conclusion to something sensible. So you start with an automatic negative like this: "I see a cloud in the sky! That means there's going to be a thunderstorm and I'm going to die." And you change it to something like this: "Just because there's a cloud in the sky doesn't mean there's going to be a thunderstorm and I'm going to die."

TOOL #7 – *Standing Up to the Bully in Your Mind*

In her book *Freeing Your Child From Anxiety* (2004), Tamar E. Chansky offers the idea that a child can use Boss Back Talk to give him the upper hand and let the fears know who's the boss. This is a great tool to use in combination with Tool #6 – Just Because. Chansky gives this example: "Just because I feel funny doesn't mean I'm in danger. If elevators weren't safe no one would use them! I'm not listening to you [to the worry]. Just because something could go wrong, doesn't mean it will. I'm not going to walk up five flights just because the elevator could break. If it happens, I'll deal with it." I would add that the words the child uses are less important than the tone. If you get your child to use the Boss Back Talk approach, have him speak to his fears in a bossy tone, really letting the fear or worry know who's in charge. What is intimidating is not so much *what* is said, but *how* it is said. A child can use this advantage when talking to an aspect of himself that he wants to control.

TOOL #8 – *The Worry Box*

This is one of the most useful tools I have found to help kids gain some control over their internal experiences. It's the children's version of the adult strategy of compartmentalization. As a grown up, you go through many times when you simply have to discipline yourself and put something out of your mind. You might have a sick child at home but also many crucial items which need your attention at your job. You make all the appropriate arrangements for your child's care, but to

some extent you need to shelve the worries
about her health, and focus on your job.
Or, it might be the opposite. You may have
some difficulties arising at your job, but
when you come home, you say to yourself,
"I'm simply not going to worry about that
problem now. I can't do anything about it
until tomorrow, so right now I'm going to
focus on helping my son with his homework." The latter might be a bit easier than

the former, but to the extent that you can do this compartmentalizing
trick, you will be more successful both at parenting and at your job.

Children need to learn to compartmentalize, but as we saw in
Chapter 2, children think more concretely than adults and therefore
need a concrete tool to accomplish this important mental task. Many
books on anxiety in children suggest you use the Worry Box. Some
suggest that children can simply draw a picture of a box. I prefer to ask
the children to actually make a box. Recycle a shoe box or some other
cardboard box and ask your child to decorate it. Then, whenever there
are worries or concerns, your child can write those worries on a piece
of paper or draw a picture of the worry, and put it into the box. Now
it's somewhere else instead of in her mind.

Ask your child where she'd like to keep the box. Some kids are
comfortable leaving the box in their room. Others want to lock it away
in the closet. Still others want it as far away from them as possible. It
doesn't matter where the box is kept.

Let your child know that the worries might sneak out of the box,
but if this happens, she can simply tell the worries to "Get back in the
box where you belong!" This is a similar process to what you might do
at home when those worries about your job slip into your conscious-
ness. If you're intent on compartmentalizing effectively, you simply
direct them to the internal shelf. You might say to yourself something
like, "I'll deal with you tomorrow when I have time."

Children typically love to do this intervention. It gives them something concrete to work with. It's a good feeling to take those worries

and put them somewhere. I usually tell them that they can go get the worry anytime they want to think about those things. It's not as though they've been erased forever. Children often bring their worry boxes to our sessions so we can see if there are any practical solutions to any of those worries. When I get a peek inside the boxes, I am often amazed at the kinds of things children worry about.

TOOL #9 – *Sing a Happy Song*

Many children respond more to music than to words or art. Music and melody are known to affect people's mood. When someone is anxious, it's as if a worried song is playing in their mind. The Happy Song approach uses the power of song to alter your emotional state. Try singing out the thoughts and feelings to a little tune: "Oh my, oh my, what's going to happen now? Will I fall? Will I look like a fool? Or will I stand tall? And make everyone drool?" When I was young, many years ago, I used to sing "I Whistle a Happy Tune" from *The King and I*, and it would give me courage. It's a simple tune with a powerful message that children can learn.

> Whenever I feel afraid
> I hold my head erect
> And whistle a happy tune,
> So no one will suspect
> I'm afraid.
>
> While shivering in my shoes
> I strike a careless pose
> And whistle a happy tune,
> And no one ever knows
> I'm afraid
>
> The result of this deception
> Is very strange to tell,
> For when I fool the people I fear
> I fool myself as well!

I whistle a happy tune,
And every single time
The happiness in the tune
Convinces me that I'm
Not afraid!

Make believe you're brave
And the trick will take you far;
You may be as brave
As you make believe you are.
You may be as brave
As you make believe you are.

TOOL #10 – *Facing Your Fears*

This is also known as Exposure Therapy, and people have been using it for years in an intuitive, non-scientific way. The gist of it is "Whatever you are afraid of … just do it!" In years gone by, if a child was afraid of the water, someone might have picked him up and thrown him in the water, forcing him to swim to shore. If he survived, he would realize there was nothing to be afraid of. If a child was afraid of the dark or the cellar, someone would lock him down there for a while to face his demons and realize that he could survive the experience. This approach actually did work for some children because going through the fire of their fears and coming out the other side actually did prove to them that the feared object or event would not kill them. Many other children, however, were severely traumatized by this kind of treatment.

Psychology teaches that children can learn from gradual and repeated exposure to a feared object or event. What is recommended is that a hierarchy of severity of fear is created, with a very low level anxiety event at the bottom of the hierarchy, leading up to the most feared object at the top. For example, if a child is afraid of dogs, at the bottom of the hierarchy might be looking at a picture of a dog. The next rung might be seeing a movie about a dog. Moving up the hierarchy, the dog might be more active and behaving in an aggressive manner. At the top of the list is encountering a growling dog, unleashed and baring his teeth. A child is thus gradually introduced to varying degrees of fear and guided, through the use of tools, to keep his heart rate and breathing calm during the experience. In a gradual way, he or she is able to experience the feared object in the absence of fear. As he or she masters each level, a reward is given.

TOOL #11 – *Getting the Upper Hand*

Using this tool is meant to help your child take charge of the situation and learn to master his or her anxieties. In fact, it's not just a single tool – it's really a whole collection of similar ones. I'm sure you and your child will discover your own variations, but to start with, here are a few you might like to try:

- **Creating a Competition: Fear vs. Fun – Who Will Win?** Every day, keep a record of how often fear wins and how often fun wins. Keep a chart, so that over time you can see whether fear is out in front or if fun is overtaking fear.

- **Becoming an Expert.** Become an expert on the thing you fear. Whether it's spiders or storms, get on the internet and find out everything you can about whatever is it you are afraid of. The more you know, the more you'll feel you're on top of things and therefore the less you'll be afraid. Knowledge is power!

- **Be Your Fear for Halloween.** The costumes children wear on Halloween often represent the things people fear the most, like ghosts, goblins and ghoulish figures. By putting on the costumes, we thumb our noses at these frightening creatures. We say, "I'm not afraid of you! I can be as scary as you! So there!" If your child can be a spider for Halloween, he may be able to show those spiders who's boss!

- **Just Change the Channel!** If you don't like what you're watching on TV, you just change the channel. Easy – we all know how to do that! Well, you can also change the movie in your mind. Just think of it as changing the channel or putting in a new DVD.

- **Just Say No!** Perhaps your child already says no if his friends want to watch a scary movie on TV or at the theatre. Explain that in the same way, he can simply say no to the scary movies in his mind.

- **Something to Think About.** Very often just saying no isn't enough. As we saw in Chapter 3, the imagination doesn't like to be bored, any more than your child himself does. So encourage your child to give his imagination something to think about, something that's really fun, like planning a birthday party or a sleepover. The topic is for your child to choose, but it should be exciting enough to keep his imagination occupied. The important thing is that your child is making the decision, that he's the one in charge and *not* his run-away imagination.

- **Get Rid of That Monster!** A technique borrowed from Barbara Coloroso, who has written many books on parenting, is to "use your imagination to turn the scary things into something more be-nign." Barbara suggests that if you have an image stuck in your mind from a nightmare or if it's just something created by your imagination, you can use your imagination either to destroy it or to turn it into something silly. For example, if a monster is chasing you, and in your mind you're running for your life, you can decide to shrink the monster, or to flush it down the toilet, or to put it in a garbage bag and throw it in the lake, or whatever your imagination decides would be an interesting and effective way to dispose of it.

  Recently I used this approach with a five-year-old girl, whose monster was preventing her and the entire family from getting to sleep at night. I said, "What would you like to do to this monster? Put it in a garbage bag and throw it in the garbage?" In a very empathetic tone she answered, "Oh, no. That would be mean." I said, "Oh, so you kind of like this monster?" "Yes," she said. So I then used the next technique, which is…

- **Draw the Scary Thing.** This is great if the scary thing is something that can be drawn easily, like a monster. I use this technique in my practice, and you can certainly use it at home. Encourage your child to draw by saying "Draw it for me. I want to know as much as I can so we can get it out of your life."

  It is difficult for me to describe in words the wonderful drawings that I've seen children create in my office. I always urge the parents to join me in marvelling at the child's imaginative capacity and creativity. "Look what you created! That's wonderful! How did you come up with that?" This way the child understands clearly that she is the author of this creation. She can change it or do whatever she wants with it, and so there's no reason to be afraid any more.

Chapter 8

Especially for kids, part 1

Welcome to a chapter that is filled with Good News About You! You are in for an exciting read, because you're about to learn some things about you that you never expected. I am guessing that you may not even want to read this book, that your mom or dad is pushing you to read it. Maybe your mom or dad is reading it with you right now. Maybe you're just going along with it, so you can get back to the things you really want to do, like playing video games or talking to your friends or texting them, but I promise you that reading this book is going to change your life in ways you can't even imagine. So, congratulations for being here! Something exciting is in store for you.

You're going to need to be a little bit patient. Before I tell you the really exciting stuff, the stuff that will change your life, there are some important things we need to discuss.

What makes up the world?

Take a look around the world you live in. You will see many different kinds of things. Some are things made by people, buildings for example – your school, your house and the place where your mom or dad work. There are also machines in the world, like the cars people drive or the stove and fridge in your kitchen. Your television, PlayStation, Xbox or DS are also all machines. All of those are what we call "inanimate," which means they are not alive, in the same way that rocks aren't alive.

When you look around the world you also see things that are alive, such as animals. We call living beings "animate." There are many thousands of different kinds of animals on the planet. There are dogs and cats and birds, animals that you might see in people's homes. But there are also animals that live in jungles like tigers, or on grasslands like lions and cheetahs. Some animals such as whales and dolphins live in the ocean. And, of course, there are all the bugs and crawly things. We could go on and on, naming thousands of different animals and where they live.

One kind of animal on our planet is called a human being or a person. You and I and all the people you know are human beings, or "humans" for short. Humans are like other animals in that we are all alive. We all breathe and need food and water. But to be a human is very special, because humans have some talents and skills that other animals don't have. For sure, animals have some talents that humans don't have. For instance, I don't think there's a human

alive who can roar as loud as a tiger, or run as fast as a cheetah. But the thing that makes humans special is our brains. Humans don't have the biggest brains of all the animals. A whale brain, for example, is much larger than a human brain. But a human brain can do some things that no other animal on the planet can do. Can you guess what those things are?

How are humans different from other animals?

There are many things that your brain can do that the brains of other animals can't do. The only animal I know of that can read a book is a human. Humans are the only ones that can count to 100 or do division. No animal, except a human, has ever built a computer or played a computer game. But I want to talk with you about one thing that your brain can do that no other animal's brain can do.

The very special thing that only human brains can do is imagine things that aren't there. For example, you can say to yourself, "I'm going to imagine that I can fly." Then you can close your eyes and picture yourself flying across the room. Imagine that! Of course you can't really fly. But even though you can't really do it, you can still imagine yourself flying. How can it be possible that you can imagine things that you have never done and could never possibly do? If you wanted to, you could even imagine yourself flying out of your house and over the moon. You could soar with the eagles – but only in your imagination, of course. What an amazing gift we humans have in our ability to imagine whatever we want. There really is no limit to what your imagination can dream up.

If you are reading this book, I have a very strong hunch that you already know a lot about the imagination. You have probably spent a lot of time playing with all the creations of your imagination. You may have spent hours and even days making up stuff, pretending about imaginary lands, imaginary people, making up imaginary stories. You may have done this by yourself or invited friends, babysitters, or even brothers, sisters, your mom or dad to join you in the places where your imagination has taken you. Playing with your imagination can be a lot of fun and a lot of fun to share with others.

Where did your imagination come from?

Sometimes wonderful things just arrive in our lives and we're not sure where they came from or why they are there. Maybe some new toy appeared in your room and you enjoyed playing with it, but your mom or dad had to remind you, maybe more than once, that your new toy came from an aunt or uncle or grandparent who lives far away. You were just busy enjoying the toy and not caring too much where it came from or why it arrived. Well, your imagination is very much like that new toy – it's really a gift. Even if you are one of those kids who likes spending time playing in the world that imaginations create, you may not have taken the time to think much about your imagination. But it's a really important part of you, and it's going to be with you for a long, long time. It's unlikely that you're going to grow tired of it, and you couldn't possibly break it, as you might break a new toy. Because it's so important, I think it's worth taking some time to think about it. Why do humans have the ability to imagine?

What is an imagination good for?

You've already discovered that it's fun to play with your imagination. But there are other reasons why it's important to have an imagination. The first reason is that sometimes what is going on around you is kind of boring, like when adults are talking to each other, and you don't even know what they're talking about, or why they're talking about it for so long. That's a good time to say to your imagination, "Let's make up a story or create an interesting circus with many different acts, or even imagine ourselves practicing something we're trying to learn, like how to hit a baseball or hockey puck, or skip rope." Imagination is a way to get away from something boring and into something that's more interesting. The boring thing is still happening, but you're not paying much atten-

tion to it, so you're not bored by it. You're involved in whatever your imagination has created, and you're enjoying that activity instead.

There's another reason why it's important to have an imagination. Sometimes what is happening in your life is actually unpleasant or even painful. This happens when you're sick or have been injured. You might have a fever or a tummy ache, or maybe you have fallen off your bike and skinned your knee. Let's imagine one of these situations. Let's say you hurt your knee. After you have had a nasty spill, you would probably limp home and ask for some help, or you might take care of the wound yourself. Let's say you've done all the right things. You washed it out really well, used some cream so that it won't get infected, and put a Band-Aid on it. But it still hurts and you're sitting there wincing in pain.

Well, this is a time to call in the imagination. If you just let your mind focus on your pain, then you'll do nothing but sit and cry and feel the pain. But you could decide to spend some time in your imagination, in a place where there is no pain. You could pretend to be somebody else, or you might use your dolls or action figures to help you pretend. Even if you're stuck in bed, your mind can imagine doing fun things. While you're spending time in your imaginary place, you might find that you don't notice the pain quite so much.

What else can your imagination do for you? Your imagination can think up new possibilities for you. For example, your mom might say, "What do you want to do to celebrate your birthday," or "What do you want to do for fun this Saturday?" If you have a good imagination, you can come up with lots of interesting ideas. Now,

some of them may be great ideas, but not really possible because they're too expensive or too difficult. You might decide you'd like to ride a rocket ship to the moon, but your mom is likely to nix that one. By the way, if she says *Yes* give me a call, because I'd like to join you! Sad to say, unless you have many millions of dollars, that one is probably not going to happen. So, your imagination will have to come up with a different idea that is more within your family budget. You might get an idea for something to build or decide to take a trip to the park.

Imaginations also play a big part every time someone simply talks to you. Think about it. The only reason you understand what someone else is talking about is that you're actually imagining what he or she is saying as it is spoken. Let's say your friend is telling you about a movie he saw. He describes it for you, using words to tell you what he saw on the screen. You understand the words because your imagination takes the words and creates a movie in your mind, so that you can kind of see the movie that your friend saw.

Of course it won't be exact, because your friend can't possibly describe absolutely everything he saw. He might leave some stuff out – he might not tell you the colours in the room in the movie or what the trees looked like. Your imagination may make up its own colours or it might simply leave the trees out. When you see the actual movie it might not be exact, but it will be close, especially if your friend was good at describing and your imagination was good at taking the words and re-creating what the words said. If you have a great imagination, the movie in your imagination might even be more interesting than the actual one!

You can see from all this that the imagination is quite amazing and important, too. Now I want you to think about the imagination in a different way.

Your life as a journey

Let's start by thinking about your life as a journey that takes many, many years. You start out as a tiny baby, then you become a bigger kid, then a teenager, then a grown-up and then an old person. It's going to be a long and very exciting journey. There are many things you will need for this journey. The first thing you need for this journey is your body. Your body is like the car that you travel in when you go somewhere with your family or other adults. It's the vehicle that you will ride in for the whole trip of your life. Your body will change as the journey progresses. Your body certainly doesn't look exactly like it did when you were a little baby, but it's still the same body, only bigger and stronger.

You have to take care of your body!

If your body is your "car," and if it's going to take you on a long journey, then it will need to be taken care of. That's one of your main jobs – to take care of your body. You know that your mom or dad has to take care of the family car, filling it up with gas and taking it to the garage for servicing once in a while. Well, you have been given a body for the trip of your life, and so you also have to take care of it. You take care of it by giving it sleep when it's tired, food when it's hungry, and taking it to the doctor when it's sick. Of course, there is more to you than just your body. In a way, you could say that you *are not* your body. But you *have* a body, and your body can do a lot of different things for you.

What are all the different things your body does for you? Sometimes it simply gets you where you want to go – it walks you down the street or runs you around the block. Your body can also learn to do really neat things like skate, ski, ride a bike or skateboard, and play different games like dodge ball or soccer. Your body doesn't know how to do these things right away – it takes practice. And so you work at it – you follow instructions and you don't give up. Usually you can get the hang of it, and that's when you and your body start having fun. When you are learning a new skill, your body won't do anything unless you tell it to. You have to be in charge of it. In a way, *you* are the boss of your body.

However, there are some things your body does without your telling it to, like breathing and keeping your temperature the same. Thank goodness! Can you imagine having to tell your body to breathe every time you needed to take in some oxygen? It would hardly leave you time to think about anything else! You'd have to say, "Breathe in now," and a moment later, you'd have to say, "Breathe out now!" Can you imagine how boring that would be? But your body is very smart, and it has a built-in way to breathe automatically, without being told.

You can probably think of many things in your house that are automatic, just like your breathing. For example, your alarm clock goes off automatically, and the furnace keeps the house warm. A long time ago, it took a lot of work to keep the house warm. When the fire in the furnace went down, people had to put more coal on to make the fire bigger again and keep everyone from freezing. Nowadays most people have furnaces that don't need this much attention, so that you and your family can do other things and still stay warm in the winter. Your body is like a modern-day furnace that does a lot of stuff automatically.

The gift of feelings

Okay, so what else are you given for the journey of your life? You're given feelings! So many different feelings! Some feelings are great, for example when we are happy, joyful or pleasantly surprised. Some feelings aren't that great, when we are worried, scared, sad, angry or guilty. Some feelings can be a bit confusing, a mixture of good and bad. Here's an example of that kind of confusing mixture: some kids might feel good when they feel angry, because anger makes some people feel strong and powerful.

HAPPY

SAD

SURPRISED

ANGRY

When we were talking about your body, we said that you *have* a body, but you *are not* your body. It's the same with feelings: you *have* feelings, but you *are not* your feelings. Also, just as you have to take care of your body, so you also have to take care of your feelings. If you don't like some of your feelings, there are ways to change them. You can cheer yourself up when you're feeling sad. You can find ways to solve your problems when you're angry about something. Sometimes you can enjoy your feelings or just allow your feelings to be there, or sometimes, if you want to, you can change them.

What do our feelings do for us? We have feelings so that we can learn about ourselves and our world. If we have a lot of good feelings when we're with someone, that usually means we like that person and probably want to find ways to be with them even more of the time. You might want to ask him or her to be your friend, so that you can spend more time together.

On the other hand, if you have a lot of bad feelings when you're with someone, those feelings might be telling you that something is wrong and needs to be fixed. Anger is a very important emotion that tells us that something is unfair or not right. It's important to pay attention to anger and to learn to express it in the right way. If anger is not expressed in the right way, then other people will not take you and your anger seriously. If you simply yell or hit or lose your temper, then often people will not even pay attention to *why* you're angry. They will just get angry back at you for expressing your anger in the wrong way. It's important to learn how to express anger in the right way, so that you can solve the problems in your life, and make your life better and better.

The gift of imagination

There's another very important piece of equipment that you are given for the journey of your life – that's your imagination. You are given an imagination for all the reasons I mentioned before – to get away from unpleasant things like boredom or pain, to think about new possibilities, to understand what others may have seen or experienced, or just to play and create. Do you remember that we said that you *have* a body, but you *are not* your body? It's the same with your imagination. You *have* an imagination. You *are not* your imagination. And now I'm going to tell you one of the secrets of this book – you have to be in charge of your imagination.

I keep saying that we are in charge of our bodies, feelings, and imaginations, but there are times when it doesn't feel like that's true. It seems as if other things take over and are in charge of us. Our bodies sometimes seem to make decisions on their own, like when you get a tummy ache or you can't fall asleep. You might say, "I didn't ask for this tummy ache. I don't want a tummy ache. I want to make this tummy ache go away."

Sometimes it may seem as if your imagination is in charge of you. There are times when your imagination does exactly what you want it to do, but other times it seems to go off in a direction that you did not choose, such as when you keep thinking about a ghost being under your bed or something bad happening to someone you love, like your mom or dad being in a car accident. You don't want to be thinking about these awful things, but you do. Your imagination seems to have a will of its own. But that's when you need to step in and let your imagination know who's the boss.

Sometimes your mom or dad has to step in and let you know who's the boss in your family. Pay attention to how they do it, and it might give you some ideas about how you can be the boss of your body, imagination and feelings, all of which are a part of *you*! I'm going to give you some tools and ideas for being the boss, but right now the main thing for you to know is that being in charge is a very important skill for you to have. Sometimes it comes naturally, but sometimes we have to learn how to do it properly.

Chapter 9

Especially for kids, part 2

Do you remember that I promised you some important information about you that was going to change your life? Well, here it comes!

There is a huge connection between anxiety and imagination. In a very real way, the bigger the imagination, the bigger the anxiety. Imagination is a wonderful thing, but it's usually more wonderful when it's going in a direction that you want it to go in. But sometimes it goes off in a scary direction, not exactly where you want it to go. In fact, maybe it's exactly the opposite direction! Or, you might feel okay about it at first, but it seems to get stuck in places, and even though you try to bring it back, it simply won't listen to you.

Here's how it works... Let's say you're a bit afraid of dogs. And you see a dog across the street. You're not sure, but it seems

The bigger the imagination,
the bigger the anxiety.

as if the dog is not tied up. As you walk by, the dog begins to bark
or even growl. Now, in your imagination, you might see the dog
running across the street to attack you. In your imagination, the
dog has long, sharp, curved teeth, and in your imagination it might
do some horrible things to you. Depending on how good your imagination is, you might even be bleeding, might even end up in the
hospital. In your imagination, awful things are happening – you

might lose your leg, or, heaven forbid, you might even lose your life! Why, you're getting ripped to little pieces, thrown around like a rag doll! Now, let's see what's really happening. What's really going on is that there's a dog barking at you from across the street – not nearly close enough to hurt you. In your imagination, however, it's a horrible scene and you're getting massacred. No wonder you're screaming!

If you have a powerful imagination, your imagination creates very realistic images in your mind. You don't just get a general feeling that the dog might do something bad. No, your imagination creates lots of really detailed pictures your mind: exactly what the dog is doing, exactly what that might feel like on your leg, exactly what Mom or Dad might do in reaction, and so on and so on. Now, when your imagination creates these scenes with lots and lots of specific details, your body will often react as if it were really happening.

To understand this better, think about what happens when you have a bad dream. While you're sleeping and inside the dream, it all seems very real. If it's a really bad dream, it might even wake you up. Once you're awake, you might notice that things have changed in your body. You might have a pain in the middle of your tummy. You might be sweating, and your hands or legs might be shaking. Your body is reacting as if the stuff in your nightmare was real – that a monster really was chasing you around the house, or a tree had really fallen on you, or whatever.

Now, what's actually happening is that you are tucked in bed, safe and sound! But it sure doesn't feel like you're safe. That's be-

cause your imagination has created a movie that seems so real, that your body believed it and is acting as if it were real! You need to set things straight, take charge of this situation, and start telling your body what's real and what's not real.

In the same way that your body reacts to dreams, so it often follows where your imagination leads. For example, if your imagination has an idea, like "Let's call a friend and have a play date," your body will often react with excitement or happiness, just thinking about all the fun that you're going to have. But if your imagination is drumming up a really scary scene, then your body reacts as if the scary thing were really happening. Remember that scary dog barking at you from across the street? Just seeing it might set your heart pounding! If this was really happening to you, you would want your mom or dad to rescue you, to take the dog away or get you away from it as quickly as possible. Sometimes moms or dads can rescue you, but when it's your imagination that is scaring you, then you are the best rescuer. You can do it by getting control of your imagination and steering it in a different direction.

Why you need to be in charge

Your imagination is a precious gift, and not everyone has as good an imagination as you do. When you grow up, you will likely do something creative with that powerful imagination! Right now you need to learn to be in charge of this gift. Because it's so powerful, it can be quite frightening – *if* you're not in charge of it.

Imagine that someone gave you a powerful car, like a Ferrari or a Lamborghini. What would it be like if you had a car with a lot of power, but no brakes or no steering wheel? Let's imagine that you are driving along and all of a sudden you come upon a large boulder in the middle of the road. If you had no brakes or steering wheel, you'd either just hope for the best, or maybe you'd jump out and let the car crash. Either way, it would be a disaster. However, cars do have brakes and steering wheels, and people have to learn how to use them before they're allowed to drive by themselves.

Maybe you've learned to ride a bicycle. Your bike also has brakes, as well as handle bars for steering. If you're heading for something bad, you brake or steer around it. If you're riding a horse, you have reins, which tell the horse which way to go and who's in charge. Your imagination is a lot like a car or a bike or a horse. Your imagination is wonderful if you know how to brake it and steer it, or have reins to control it, but it can be a source of trouble if it is totally in charge and you are simply along for the ride.

By now you are probably putting a lot of this information together and figuring out that the reason that you have more of what we call "anxiety reactions" is that you also have more imagination than others. If you have made that connection – congratulations! You are absolutely right! Every person is unique and special in his or her own way. Everyone has different gifts. Some people have longer legs so they can run faster. Other may have nimble fingers so they can play a musical instrument or really good ears that understand how notes make up a song.

You are one of the people lucky enough to have a really great imagination. This means that your brain is able to create more detailed and colourful pictures in your head. This is truly a wonderful gift that you have been blessed with! I hope you realize how truly amazing and wonderful this gift is and how much fun you will have with it throughout the entire journey of your life, as well as how much pleasure you might bring to others along the way. Maybe you will spend some time just marvelling at this powerful gift you have at your disposal and at the many different things it creates in your life. The more you know about your imagination, the easier will be the job of being in charge.

If your imagination has been getting out of control lately and taking you to uncomfortable or scary places, then it's time to do something about that. It's time to learn how to tame this force so that you can truly enjoy it as it was meant to be enjoyed. Maybe it's not such a bad thing that your imagination has sometimes got out of control, because now you can appreciate its amazing power. It's important to respect power. We respect the power of fire, for example, but we have to learn how to handle it. We know that if used properly it can cook our food and keep us warm, but if used improperly it can cause a lot of destruction. Your imagination is a lot like that. It has the power to create good in your life, and also to create trouble for you.

Learning how to be in charge

Are you ready to learn how to be in charge? We are going to use the power of your imagination to learn how to tame that imagination. Ready? Let's begin…

Let's pretend that your imagination is a horse that you have to learn to tame, to let it know that you're in charge of it. What does your horse look like? What colour is she? Does she have a name? What other details come to your mind when you think about your horse?

So, let's imagine you're on top of that horse, but you can't find the reins. The reins have fallen down, and you're in the saddle but have no way to tell the horse which way you want it to go. Your horse

sees something interesting and bolts over to see what it is. Now your horse gets frightened by a loud sound and is running in all different directions at once. Without the reins, your only choice is to hang on with all your might and try hard not to fall off. All you can do is hope your horse gets tired and calms down soon. You might think to yourself, "I don't know if I can continue to hold on. I wish she would get tired already. I'm getting tired of hanging on." You might talk to your horse, but if it's really frightened or curious about something your horse will probably not pay much attention to you.

Now, imagine that you remember that the reins are within your reach. So, you lean down and grab them. Now you can pull back hard and tell your horse firmly that you are in charge and that you want her to slow down right now. Horses are living things and if this is the first time you are riding this horse, she still might not listen to your commands. Horses need to be tamed. Once they are tamed, they understand that the person riding them, the person holding the reins, is in charge. Then they will obey the person in charge. In order to win the horse's respect, the person in charge has to be firm, but not mean. There are right and wrong ways to handle the reins. The rules about taming something are fairly simple.

Rule #1 — The command you give should be short and clear. Use the same command each time.

Rule #2 — Don't fight with your horse. If you get angry at the horse, it's likely the horse will get angry back. Then you're no better off than you were when it was galloping off where you didn't want to go, and you had no say in the matter.

You might be asking at this point, how do I tame my horse? How do I get to the point where the horse knows that I'm the boss? That's a very good question. Have you ever tamed anything? Have you ever housebroken a family pet, like the dog, teaching him to pee and poop outside and not on the carpet? Have you ever taught a younger brother or sister, around the age of two, not to touch dangerous things like electrical outlets or sharp objects likes knives or scissors? If you have, then you know that what you do is to tell them, over and over and over and over, "No, no, no, no, no, no…," and then point them in the right direction. In the case of the puppy, you bring him to a piece of newspaper, giving him clear directions to poop or pee there. Eventually, you might bring the newspaper outside, so he gets the idea that outside is the proper place for this activity.

With the toddler, you might distract her from the dangerous activity by directing her to play with something safe, or getting her to be interested in something entertaining that you are doing, like making a weird face or a strange noise. This is called "redirection," and it has to be done many, many times, but eventually the puppy or the toddler gets the idea of what is acceptable and what is not. It's important not to be too harsh with either the puppy or the toddler, or they will develop a very nasty manner, because they will be very angry at being mistreated. But if you are firm but respectful, and keep repeating the command, then they will learn how to behave properly and spend many years being very happy in their lives.

This may seem like a tough job. You might think that it's too hard and you just don't feel up to it. Well, you're partly right. It's not easy, but it has to be done, and I know that you *are* up to it! Teaching a toddler to stay away from dangerous things isn't easy. Training a dog to do his business outside and not inside isn't easy. But I think everyone agrees these are necessary if the dog is going to live indoors with the family, and if the toddler is going to survive to get to grade one. Sometimes jobs are not easy, but they are very worthwhile and once they are done, there's a lot of enjoyment to be had.

Taming your imagination is not easy, but I know you can do it. It's something you will not have to do completely on your own, although it *is* your imagination, and ultimately *you* are the one who needs to be in charge. Every kid has at least one parent to help them learn how to be a successful human being. So you do have someone

to help you. There's another thing that makes training your imagination easier than, say, training a puppy – it's actually part of you, so
it can understand you better than a puppy can.

Why do kids have parents?

At times, you may have asked yourself this question, especially
when your mom or dad is telling you for the millionth time to do
something you really don't want to do. Since we've been talking
about horses and dogs, let's go back to them. If you were born a
puppy, you'd be ready to leave your mom by the time you were a
few weeks or maybe a few months old. That's because it only takes
a few weeks for a puppy to learn everything it needs to learn about
how to be a successful dog. There's not that much that puppies
need to learn. They need to learn how to eat and sleep and run and
where to pee and poop (they already know how!). Foals (which is
what we call baby horses) leave their moms when they're between
four and six months old. Can you imagine leaving your mom at that
age? Not likely!

If you're a human, there is lots and lots to learn. Most humans
stay with their parents for at least eighteen years, sometimes longer.
It would take pages and pages to list all the things humans have to
learn. First you have to learn to use your arms and legs properly,
then to speak the language that the people around you speak, then
to read, and possibly sing songs and play all the games that the
people in your life play. Then you go to school and start learning to

THUMP

BUMP

Into the big world

read and write, do math, learn about the world around you, and so much more. You also have to learn how to ride a bike, and possibly do other sports, so that you can play with others who like doing those things. Then there are all the things that adults do, like work and manage money, and drive cars or trucks or fly planes, and cook meals and take care of people when they're sick. The list goes on and on. If there weren't so much to learn, kids might be more like puppies or foals and leave home at just few weeks or months of age, as soon as they were strong enough and had learned the basics. But that's not how it is for kids.

It's important to let your parents help you while you're young, so that you're not trying to do all this by yourself. There will be some stuff you learn on your own. There's other stuff they can help you learn. And there's also some stuff they have learned and can teach you, so that you don't have to spend time learning it on your own, giving you more time to learn new stuff. That way you will know all the stuff that they know plus all the stuff you learned on your own and become even smarter than your parents when you grow up. Believe it or not, that's what your mom and dad really want for you. The more you learn and know, the more fun you will have in your life. That way you can be really smart and competent, and be the really super kid you want to be!

You already have many skills!

Let's think back to all the things you've already learned how to control in your life. Everyone has a few. You may have learned to ride a two-wheeler. You may have learned to master ice skates, skis, a hockey stick or a baseball bat. You may have learned to swim or dive or to whistle or to blow bubbles with gum. There are many, many things that we must learn to master. Whatever you put your mind to learning, it probably required a lot of repetition and patience. Whatever skills you developed in mastering those other things, you're going to use in mastering your imagination. And just as once you had learned those other things they seemed so easy, so it will also be easy to control your imagination once you have learned how. As I describe the process of mastering your imagination, I hope it will remind you of your successes in other areas.

How to be in charge

 First, always know that *you* are in charge, that you hold the reins. If you don't know that you're in charge, your imagination will never know it.

 Second, be clear where you want your imagination to go. Of course, you know where you *don't* want it to go. You don't want it to be thinking about dog attacks, or other scary things. So you clearly say *No!* to those things. But you also need to steer your imagination in some other direction. Just as you directed the little toddler to play with something safer than an electrical outlet, give your imagination something else to think about besides the scary thing.

 Third, have a basket of things for your imagination to focus on before it gets into trouble with something frightening. Why do you need a basket of interesting activities? Well, your imagination is a lot like you in many key ways. One way is that just like you, what your imagination hates most of all is being bored.

Don't let your imagination get bored

Most kids hate being bored. I know many kids who would prefer fighting with their brothers or sisters and even getting in trouble with their parents because it's better than being bored. Kids and imaginations really hate it when nothing is happening. It's important to understand this about imaginations, because if you take the scary things out of your imagination, but don't replace them with something better, your imagination is likely to want to return to the scary thing because at least it's not boring.

What sorts of activities can you use to keep your imagination busy? For example, you might have an ongoing creative project that you're working on. You might be creating a circus, or a movie about pirates. When your imagination is lured into creating a scary movie and you don't want to go there, then talk to your imagination much the same way you'd talk to your little brother or sister. You say, "No, no, no, no, no," to your imagination, "let's think about that pirate movie instead."

Here's another strategy. Suppose you're trying to learn a new sport, like tennis or skiing. You can distract a runaway imagination by simply taking a few minutes to go over in your mind how to do your new sport. This is a fabulous way to spend time because the more you practice in your imagination, the better you will actually become.

The imagination can be used for fun!

Congratulations!

You have now learned quite a lot about the imagination. You've learned that your powerful imagination is a wonderful gift that makes you special. You've learned why you have an imagination and how it can be used for fun or misery, how there is a connection between the powerful anxiety you experience sometimes and your powerful imagination. Believe it or not, just having this new understanding will make a difference – it will give you a real advantage in the process of taming your imagination.

What happens now? Well, you need to practice being in charge of this great gift, your imagination. This book has given you some tools to help you take charge. You need to keep practicing those tools and keep reminding yourself of what you've learned here. It will likely take lots of time and hard work, but you should never give up. The more you work at it, the stronger you will become and the more you will be in control of yourself.

For a creative person like you, this book is just the starting point. I'm sure you can come up with exciting new tools of your own to help you master your imagination. If you are willing to share some of your ideas, I'd love to hear from you, so that other kids can benefit from them. My website is **www.docrobin.com**, and you can contact me there. The process of learning to be the master of your imagination is rewarding and fun, but don't expect it all to happen in a day or even a week. Enjoy and celebrate your successes along the way! Always remember – you're in good company.

Chapter 10

Why it doesn't always work

I HAVE FOUND that while my method works well for many children, there are a few for whom it is not effective. I've given considerable thought to those cases. It seems to me that the failures fall into two different categories: cases in which the child does not really want a change and cases in which the parents have not pushed hard enough for a change.

What can you do when the method explained in this book doesn't seem to help? First, you need to think hard about what the child and the parent really want. Second, you may need to seek other approaches.

What does the child really, really want?

SOMETIMES KIDS ARE SIMPLY NOT VERY MOTIVATED to make a change. They would rather continue doing what they know than have to learn some completely new way of doing things, which might involve giving up some of the benefits that come from having anxiety. This is what psychologists refer to as secondary gain, and, as you will recall, we touched on it briefly in Chapter 7. Here I'd like to go into it in more detail.

Anxiety comes in many degrees of severity. Sometimes it is uncomfortable but tolerable. Sometimes it can be very intense and debilitating, causing the child to have severe stomach pains and even to throw up. Physical symptoms aside, what often makes anxiety intolerable is the price that is paid in missing the good things in life.

Natalie was a bright and delightful eleven-year-old girl whose anxiety was about all the scary things in the woods: germs and wildlife with which she was unfamiliar. Her parents and siblings enjoyed going on outings in the woods and Natalie was frequently left behind. Although her family would beg and plead with her to join them, more often than not she would choose to stay behind. Sometimes that meant that Mom or Dad stayed with her, and then she felt guilty about causing her parent to miss out on the fun as well. Natalie was highly motivated to make some changes. When she first came to see me she had been missing out on family excursions for years, but she didn't like missing out and didn't want either of her parents to miss out either. Natalie responded very quickly to the tools given her and soon made enormous changes. Within a few sessions, she was fully participating in all family outings, going on hikes in the woods and even enjoying them.

Max was a different story. He was an adorable and precocious eight-year-old with many anxieties, including robbers or bad guys coming into the house at night and killing everyone. This necessitated having his mother sit with him for hours while he fell asleep. Often in the middle of the night Max would end up either sleeping next to his mother or on the floor beside his parents' bed. Max wasn't really missing out on anything. He was managing to get enough sleep, either with a parent beside him in his own room or in his parents' room. He did extremely well in school, and was fully engaged in life, with many friends. He also got along well with all of his siblings. I could tell from the mom's expression how much she adored her son.

When asked directly, Max said he wanted to "not be scared of robbers," but when given tools to make changes, he insisted none of them would work. When his mother was questioned about how big a problem it was for her that she had to sit with Max for an hour or more to get him to sleep, the mother replied, "I don't mind." When asked how big a problem it was that Max ended up in her bed, she said, "I know

he'll grow out of it eventually." When asked why she had come for help, she said, "I'm worried about Max's future. I don't want him to be so fearful when he grows up."

But Max himself lacked sufficient motivation to make a change. Although his mother asked me for some concrete tools that would take away his fears, neither she nor Max were concerned enough about the problem *in the present* to make sufficient effort to bring about a change. Max was managing his anxiety well enough, and it wasn't causing any negative effects in his life at the present time. Neither his mother or father were angry or even irritated with him. His mother seemed to enjoy their intimate and lengthy good night rituals and didn't really mind waking up in the middle of the night to find Max there. She was very tolerant and forgiving. Max's daily life was rich with activity and positive relationships with others. He was very creative and enjoyed his life immensely. At a very real level there was no reason to make any changes. The main reason the mother sought help for Max was hypothetical – what if this causes problems for him in the future? The present is fine, but what about tomorrow? Max himself would wonder, "What if I try all these things and they don't work?" But he didn't actually want to try them.

What does the parent really, really want?

MANY OF THE PARENTS WHO SEEK HELP from me suffer from guilt feelings for various reasons, and this affects their behaviour towards their children. In my opinion, one of the reasons for this is that many parents are working harder and for longer hours than ever before. They are therefore less inclined to set limits on their children's behaviour or push their children to do the things they need to do but do not want to do, like getting to bed on time, or putting away their video games and doing their homework. Many parents feel that their children are being shortchanged, that the children receive too little of their parents' attention, affection and time. To compensate for the long hours they spend at work, the parents indulge their children with material goods and later bed times. What's more, many people have a hard time establishing boundaries between family time and work time. When work-related problems intrude on family time, it is the children who suffer the most, as parents are well aware.

I have come to appreciate over the years that children often intuitively understand the connection between time and money. When they see that adults must spend their time working in order to earn money, they reach the conclusion that Time = Money. First and foremost, children want their parents' time and attention, but if denied this, they will opt for what they see as equivalent – they will begin to demand things, which cost money. This makes them feel that they are loved and valued. I have talked to hundreds of children who verbalize this with statements such as "I wish my Mom didn't have to work" and "If only Dad would spend more time with us."

Children who present with anxiety symptoms are often clearly lobbying for attention rather than things. A child's fears and anxieties and his demands for a parent's attention do seem to trump all other matters. Thus children hang on to their anxieties in order to override the priorities set by their parents. A parent in this situation often concludes, "If I hadn't been so involved in my work and had given him a bit more of my time, he might not have been so fearful at this age. He might have gotten over it by now. It's all my fault, and I'd better respond now and not leave him alone to fend for himself."

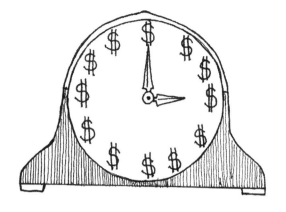

Unfortunately this is not the best solution. Encouraging anxiety only creates a strong pattern of dependent behaviour. From the child's perspective, he gets what he wants – a parent's attention. But while the parent has rescued the child by giving him comfort and reassurance, she has not encouraged self-reliance, not taught the child how to deal with fear on his own. The child has learned that the only way to deal with fear is to lure the parent away from her own activity and make the world safe once again. Moreover, in this situation, the fear is magnified, because giving in to fear always makes the fear stronger. This means that as the child grows, he will develop mechanisms for always keeping the parent nearby or, at a later stage, for connecting with the parent so the rescue mission can be conducted from afar, perhaps by cell phone. The demand for rescue becomes more insistent as the child matures and the problems to be faced become larger and even more frightening.

One family in particular taught me how the guilt mechanism can prevail in a family. Susie was a petite adorable nine-year-old girl, bright and precocious beyond her years. When she was an infant, she had a serious medical condition that remained undiagnosed for almost two years. Susie screamed in pain every night, and her mother and father were unable to calm her. Since she was their first child, they were riddled with doubt about their competence as parents. Finally a diagnosis was made, and they had a proper explanation for Susie's wailing. She had a bladder malformation and underwent several surgeries to correct it. By the time she was four years old, the physical problem had been solved, but the psychological problem of Susie refusing to sleep in her own bed persisted. She complained of many fears in the night, and this kept her entrenched in her parents' bed. The parents felt incredibly guilty that it had taken so long to pin down the cause. They felt they should have pushed the medical system harder to find the cause and should not have agreed with the doctors that it was simply a bad case of colic. Their guilt told them that they had been bad and ineffectual parents and that now they had to pay the price of never having privacy in their marital bed.

Susie, at nine, was still sleeping between her two parents, and she had no plans to move out of that comfy spot. When I asked her how old she might be when she felt she would be ready to sleep in her own bed, she emphatically informed me, "Never! I'll sleep with my parents until I get married, and then I'll have a husband to sleep with." Her parents, especially her father, looked horrified at this answer – all the colour disappeared from his face. Up till that point in treatment, none of the strategies I had offered Susie were making a difference in her behaviour, and now we all knew why. She was not motivated to make any changes. She liked that spot between her parents and slept very well there. In fact, Susie had an aunt in another part of the country who was a psychologist and who had also been offering her many good strategies, but to no avail. But Susie's statement had galvanized her father, and things were about to change.

At the next session, the father asked to speak to me alone and said, "I don't care what it takes but I want Susie in her own bed. I want my bed back. I want my marriage back. I've had enough!" I could tell that he meant what he said, and I replied that I was very happy to hear him say that. I told him that now he needed to convince Susie, and he did just that. He informed Susie of his decision, and his tone of voice and body language convinced her that he meant it. She cowered as she heard him speak. Her eyes widened at the revelation that she was going to have to find a way to manage in her own bed. She had all the strategies given to her by her parents, her psychologist aunt and me. Within a few weeks, Susie was sleeping soundly in her own bed and she was extremely proud of herself.

Until we had turned a corner, the parents' motivation for change was thwarted by their guilt, caused by having been unsuccessful in identifying a medical problem for many months. One can be very sympathetic to Susie's parents. It must have been a horrendous situation – all those sleepless nights hearing a young child screaming in pain, not knowing what was the matter. Even after they had found the cause, they spent a long time second-guessing themselves about many of the decisions they had made along the way.

Susie's parents, like many others, were aware of the need for change, but they wanted their child to be motivated to make the change herself, to understand and accept that she really ought to sleep on her own. In Susie's case, this was just not going to happen, and it left her parents in a bind. Judging from the clients in my practice, many parents of anxious children seem to be extremely kind people who don't want to cause distress in their children. If children have already had a lot of distress in their lives, then parents often don't want to be the cause of more difficulty. Susie's parents were certainly like that. They wanted to take away her pain, not be the cause of it. This tendency, however, resulted in a situation that was untenable, with Susie not sleeping in her own bed and preventing the parents from having normal marital relations. I have spoken to many parents who are in the same situation as Susie's parents, with a child sleeping in the parents' bed instead of his own. I am often amazed at the creative solutions parents find to have a sex life, such as using the bathtub, or the basement. While this may make life interesting – and it certainly attests to the parents' creativity – it is not the best solution.

Other approaches

IN WRITING THIS BOOK, I wanted to explain anxiety in a way that would be helpful to both parents and children. I also wanted to provide a framework for motivating children to make changes in their own lives. However, if the approach outlined here does not help your child become more motivated to make changes, then you will need to look elsewhere to find the reasons behind the need to hold on to the problem. It is always easier to see what's going on in other people or in other families than in ourselves or our families, and that's where the services of a professional can be very helpful. A professional – a psychologist, social worker or someone else trained in the field – can help you create a step-by-step plan that makes sense. He or she can help you discover something you may have overlooked, something that may not be obvious. As well, a professional will be able to help you appreciate when new patterns are emerging, to encourage you to persevere when you're convinced that nothing is going to help, and to offer practical suggestions that you might not have thought about yourself. At the very least, seeking professional help forces you and your child to set aside some time on a regular basis to focus on the issue and to make it a priority in your lives. Otherwise, the ordinary business of life itself tends to take over, and we forget even a worthy goal such as learning to control the imagination.

If you do decide to seek professional help for your child and if you feel that this book has been a helpful starting point, you might want to bring it along to your first appointment. It should be possible to incorporate some of the tools and strategies we have discussed into your child's plan of treatment.

And finally, there is the question of timing. If your child's imagination has been a dominant force in his or her life for many years, then it will take considerable time and effort to sort things out and put the child in charge. But if this is just not the right moment in your child's life to make changes, then all you can do for now is remain patient.

Conclusion

NOW THAT WE'VE COME TO THE END OF THE BOOK, I want to thank you for taking the time to read it. I hope that you enjoyed it, and even more importantly, I hope it allowed you to see anxiety from a different perspective. Many people start from the assumption that anxiety is something to be tackled head on, to be annihilated. But this is not a helpful approach. We need to understand that more often than not, anxiety is a product of the imagination. There's something of a paradox here: generally, we think of anxiety as a problem, while the imagination is something we admire and encourage, especially in children.

The key to understanding this puzzle is to recognize that the imagination has to be tamed or controlled, much that same way you would deal with a little puppy that wanders off into the wrong places or a small child who, in spite of our instructions, continues to do as he or she pleases. We wouldn't want to lash out at the puppy or the child, but rather to teach them to control themselves, to adapt their behaviour to our way of life. This is also how we need to deal with a wayward imagination. Once the imagination is under control, anxiety will diminish. If you can teach your child to direct the imagination in a positive way, then he or she will be at the helm of one of the most powerful cognitive mechanisms humans possess.

As with most learned skills, this mastery will not be achieved overnight. It is extremely important that you give it the respect it deserves and allow it the time it requires. If you or your child expect that this change will occur magically or instantly, then you are both likely to give up when you don't see immediate results. That would be very unfortunate. In this book, I've offered you some excellent tools for mastering the imagination, but no matter how good the tools are, it takes time for them to be incorporated into anyone's repertoire of responses. It takes many repetitions of the same action in order for the brain itself to make new pathways. That's true of athletic or musical skills, and even more so for the skill of training the imagination to follow the path you set for it.

Please don't give up, and keep encouraging your child not to give up. If you continue making the effort and do so in a loving but persistent manner, you will help your child achieve inner harmony rather than remaining at odds with key aspects of the self. For a person's psychological health, nothing is more important than this.

For further reading

Beaney, M., & Open University. (2005). *Imagination and creativity.* Milton Keynes: Open University.

> An interesting exploration of the way a number of philosophers have grappled with the issue of understanding the imagination. Discusses Descartes, Hume, Kant and Wittgenstein, among others.

Bouchard, S., St-Jacques, J., Robillard, G., & Renaud, P. (August 01, 2008). Anxiety increases the feeling of presence in virtual reality. *Presence: Teleoperators and Virtual Environments, 17, 4, 376–391.*

> An article suggesting that people with high levels of anxiety seem to have more of the quality of presence when experiencing virtual reality, which allows them to be immersed in the experience rather than to remain distant from it.

Burns, D. D. (1992). *Feeling good: The new mood therapy.* New York: Avon Books.

> An extremely well-written and helpful book on cognitive behaviour therapy. Primarily used for adolescents and adults.

Chansky, T. E. (2004). *Freeing your child from anxiety: Powerful, practical strategies to overcome your child's fears, phobias, and worries.* New York: Broadway Books.

An intelligent, well-written and comprehensive professional book on childhood anxiety. Offers insight into the problem from the child's point of view.

Clark, S. L., Garland, E. J., & Ostrom, K. J. (2009). *The kid's guide to taming worry dragons*. Vancouver, BC: Mood and Anxiety Disorder Clinic, Dept. of Psychiatry, British Columbia Children's Hospital.
A wonderful book that speaks directly to children and is full of lots of illustrations and concrete tools for gaining control. Available at http://bookstore.cw.bc.ca. The companion book for parents is listed below under Garland, E. J.

Friedberg, R. D., & McClure, J. M. (2002). *Clinical practice of cognitive therapy with children and adolescents: The nuts and bolts*. New York: Guilford Press.
A creative and easily understood approach to helping children change unhealthy ways of thinking. It is clear that the authors have worked with many children and understand the challenges of applying the techniques of cognitive behavioural therapy to children.

Garland, E. J., & Clark, S. L. (2009). *Taming worry dragons: A manual for children, parents, and other coaches*. Vancouver, BC: Mood and Anxiety Disorder Clinic, Dept. of Psychiatry, British Columbia Children's Hospital.
If you're looking for more tools and strategies to help your child, this is an excellent follow-up to *Anxiety and the Gift of Imagination*. Available at http://bookstore.cw.bc.ca. The companion book for kids is listed above under Clark, S. L.

Harris, P. L. (2000). *The work of the imagination*. Cambridge, MA: Blackwell Publishers.
A collection of brilliant articles describing his research on the development of imagination in children. Fascinating and easy to read.

Huebner, D., & Matthews, B. (2006). *What to do when you worry too much: A kid's guide to overcoming anxiety.* Washington, DC: Magination Press.
> A guide for children and parents in the use of techniques of cognitive behaviour therapy. With lively metaphors and illustrations to engage children, as well as many exercises and paper-and-pencil activities.

Manassis, K. (1996). *Keys to parenting your anxious child.* Hauppauge, NY: Barron's Educational Series.
> A reassuring manual on using behavioural approaches with children, including some cognitive behaviour therapy. Explains systematically taking children through a hierarchy of fears so that eventually they are no longer reacting with the same intensity to the feared object.

Rapee, R. M. (2000). *Helping your anxious child: A step-by-step guide for parents.* Oakland, CA: New Harbinger Publications.
> A very readable book with easy-to-use tools for establishing a comprehensive treatment plan for children.

Reznick, C. (2009). *The power of your child's imagination: How to transform stress and anxiety into joy and success.* New York: Penguin Group.
> A very clear and useful book, giving many exciting tools for helping children use their imaginations to enhance their well-being and to manage their stresses and anxieties. A perfect next step after *Anxiety and the Gift of the Imagination.*

Wagner, A. P. (2002). *Worried no more: Help and hope for anxious children.* Rochester, NY: Lighthouse Press.
> Practical guidance for parents, school personnel and health care professionals in helping children cope with many areas of anxiety.

John Strachan, 1949 – 2011

A Tribute to John Strachan

From the moment I finally tracked you down, I knew you were the right illustrator for my book. I had seen and admired your illustrations for another book, and hoped you might be interested in my project. But tracking you down turned out to be more difficult than I expected, since you had moved 4,000 kilometres across Canada and hadn't left a forwarding address. But I was determined and, thankfully, successful. When you received the initial draft of the book, you wrote to say, "I have read the book four times and it has become my bible." Right then, I knew you were the ideal person for the job.

In spite of all the health challenges you endured during our years of working together, whenever I asked you for anything, you always delivered. Your illustrations for this book speak for themselves. They are lively and whimsical and capture the concepts as if you had lived them your entire life. I am grateful to you for your work, which makes the text come alive, as well for as your enthusiasm for the project, which never waned. My only regret is that you are not here to share in the final product. I hope you are at peace wherever you are and that your loving grin is shining down on us, as our book finally becomes available to all the children who stand to benefit from it.

Robin Alter

42847209R00088

Made in the USA
Middletown, DE
23 April 2017